Botany

49 More Science Fair Projects

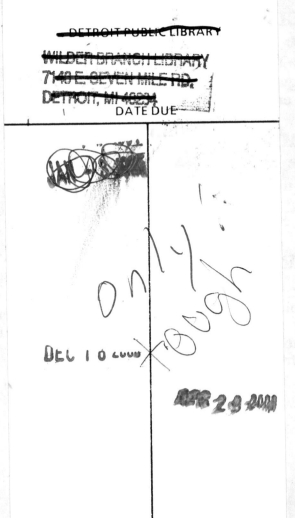

Other Books in the
Science Fair Projects Series

BOTANY:
49 Science Fair Projects (No. 3277)

This first volume in the series contains a rich source of project ideas for plant germination, photosynthesis, hydroponics, plant tropism, plant cells, seedless plants, and plant dispersal.

EARTH SCIENCE:
49 Science Fair Projects (No. 3287)

This second volume in the series concentrates on Earth's geology, meteorology, and oceanography, as well as the Earth's crust, weather, solar energy, acid rain, fossils, and rocks and minerals.

ENVIRONMENTAL SCIENCE:
49 Science Fair Projects (No. 3369)

This third volume in the series deals with Earth's surroundings and how pollution, waste disposal, irrigation, erosion and heat, and light affect the ecology.

COMPUTERS:
49 Science Fair Projects (No. 3524)

This fourth volume in the series integrates computers with science, applying scientific principals to games of chance, aircraft design, calculating energy costs, forecasting weather, calculating odds, and making mathematical conversions.

Science Fair
Projects

Series

Botany

49 More
Science Fair Projects

Robert L. Bonnet
G. Daniel Keen

TAB BOOKS
Blue Ridge Summit, PA

FIRST EDITION
FIRST PRINTING

Library of Congress Cataloging-in-Publication Data

Bonnet, Robert L.
   Botany : 49 more science fair projects / Robert L. Bonnet and G. Daniel Keen.
    p. cm.
   Includes index.
   Summary: A collection of experiments and projects in botany, focusing on germination, vegetative reproduction, hydroponics, photosynthesis, and plant stimulation, transport, and dispersal.
   ISBN 0-8306-7416-0   ISBN 0-8306-3416-9 (pbk.)
   1. Botany—Experiments—Juvenile literature. 2. Botany-
-Exhibitions—Juvenile literature. 3. Science projects—Juvenile literature. [1. Botany—Experiments. 2. Experiments. 3. Science projects.] I. Keen, Dan. II. Title.
QK52.6.B64 1990
581'.078—dc20   90-36462
                                     CIP
                                     AC

TAB BOOKS offers software for sale. For information and a catalog, please contact TAB Software Department, Blue Ridge Summit, PA 17294-0850.

Questions regarding the content of this book should be addressed to:

Reader Inquiry Branch
TAB BOOKS
Blue Ridge Summit, PA 17294-0850

Acquisitions Editor: Kimberly Tabor
Technical Editor: Lori Flaherty
Production: Katherine G. Brown
Book Design: Jaclyn J. Boone
Illustrations: Carol Chapin

Disclaimer

Adult supervision is advised when working with these projects. No responsibility is implied or taken for anyone who sustains injuries as a result of using the materials or ideas put forward in this book. Taste nothing. Use proper equipment (gloves, safety glasses, and other safety precautions). Clean up broken glass with a dust pan and brush. Use chemicals with extra care. Wash hands after project work is done. Tie up loose hair and clothing. Follow step-by-step procedures; avoid short cuts. Never work alone. Remember, adult supervision is advised. Safety precautions are addressed in the text. If you use common sense and make safety the first consideration, you will create safe, fun, educational, and rewarding projects.

Contents

Acknowledgments

We wish to extend our appreciation to the following people: George M. Keen, editorial assistance; Carl Gallela, Principal, Dennis Township School; Tom Keck, Superintendent, Belleplain State Forest; and John D. Webersinn, Webersinn's Landscaping.

Introduction

At some time during our school years, all of us have been required to do at least one science project. It might have been growing seeds in kindergarten or building a Telsa coil in high school, but such experiences are not forgotten and help shape our views of the world around us.

Doing a science project yields many benefits beyond the obvious education value. The logical process required helps encourage clear, concise thinking that can carry through a student's entire life. Science in general requires a discipline of the mind, clear notes and data gathering, curiosity and patience, an honesty regarding results and procedures, and finally, a concise reporting of the work accomplished. A student's success in a science project can provide him or her with the motivation to strive for success in other areas.

Parents are encouraged to work with their children on projects. Not only will you be fostering richer family relationships, but enhancing the child's self-esteem as well.

Finally, there is always the possibility of a spin off interest developing. For instance, a child who chooses to do a project in mathematics, perhaps using a battery, switches, and light bulbs to represent binary numbers, might discover a liking for electronics.

But where does the student, teacher, or parent look for suggestions for such projects? It is our aim to address this void by offering a large collection of projects and project ideas in a series of books.

These books target anyone who wants or needs to do a science project. A teacher might want to do classroom projects; a student might be assigned to do a project for class by a science teacher or to enter one in a science fair; a parent might want to help their child with a science fair project; and finally, a person might want to do an experiment or project just for the fun of it. Science teachers can use these books to help them conduct a science fair at their school or to suggest criteria for judging. Parents might feel apprehensive when their child comes home with a project requirement to do for school. These books will come to their rescue.

Our goal is to show you project ideas from beginning to end. Students need a starting place and direction. Questions are posed in the form of needs or problems (discovering how to get electricity from the sun was born out of a need, for example). We then provide overviews, organizational direction, suggest possible hypotheses, indicate materials, procedures, and controls. The projects explained are complete, but can also be used as spring boards from which you can create expanded projects. All projects are brainstormed for going further. You are shown how to develop ideas and projects using valid scientific processes and procedures.

This book is the second in the Science Fair Projects Series that deals with botany—the scientific study of the plant kingdom. Together, these two books offer 98 complete projects with more than 200 ideas for going further. The overwhelming interest in the first book suggested the need for more experiments.

The chapters in each book are organized by topics. Some projects might overlap into more than one science discipline as well as within that discipline. In this case, we have attempted to place the projects under the seemingly dominant theme. You can quickly skim through the topics and choose a project that interests you or suits your ability or the ability of your group.

Projects are designed to target the sixth- to ninth-grade level student, but many projects can be watered down and used for younger children. Similarly, older students can take each project's brainstormed ideas in the *Going Further* section of each project to more advanced levels.

It is very important to read the introduction at the beginning of the chapter from which you plan on doing a project. The introduction contains important information to each project in the chapter. For example, in the chapter on hydroponics, each project shows a *nutrient solution* in the materials lists, but it is not explained. The chapter introduction, however, defines this term and gives procedures for creating it. In addition, the Resources List lists suppliers where nutrient solutions and other laboratory supplies can be purchased ready-made.

After selecting a project and reading the chapter's introduction, read the entire project through carefully. This will help you understand the overall scope of the project, the materials needed, the time requirements, and the procedure before you begin.

Safety and ethics must be a consideration throughout. Some projects require cutting with a knife or scissors, and common sense usage should be practiced. Projects that *must* have adult supervision are indicated by the phrase **Adult Supervision Required** next to the title. These projects deal with caustics, poisons, acids, high temperatures, high voltages, or other potentially hazardous conditions. Ethical science concepts involve very careful considerations about living organisms. One cannot recklessly cause pain, damage, or death to any living organism.

There is no limit to the number of themes and the number of hypotheses one can form about our universe. The number is as infinite as the stars in the heavens. It is our hope that many students will take off on the ideas presented, develop their own unique hypotheses, and proceed with their experiments using accepted scientific methods.

Some projects could go on for years. There is no reason to stop a project other than getting tired of it. It might be that what you studied this year can be taken a step further next year. With each question or curiosity answered, more questions are raised. It has been our experience that answers produce new and exciting questions. We believe that science discovery and advancement proceeds as much on excellent questions as it does on excellent answers.

We hope we can stimulate the imagination and encourage creative thinking in students, teachers, parents, and others. Learning is rewarding and enjoyable. Good luck with your project!

Robert L. Bonnet
G. Daniel Keen

How to Use This Book

All projects that require adult supervision have the **STOP** symbol at the beginning of the project. No responsibility is implied or taken for anyone who sustains injuries as a result of the materials or ideas put forward in this book. Taste nothing that is not directly food related. Use proper equipment (gloves, safety glasses, and other safety equipment). Clean up broken glass with a dust pan and brush. Use chemicals with extra care. Wash hands after project work is done. Tie up loose hair and clothing. Follow step-by-step procedures; avoid short cuts. Never work alone. Remember, adult supervision is advised. Use common sense and make safety the first consideration, and you will have a safe, fun, educational, and rewarding project.

1

Science Projects

Before you begin working on a science project, there are some important things you need to know. It is important that you read this chapter before starting any of the projects in this book. It defines terms and sets up guidelines that you should adhere to as work on your project progresses.

What Is a Science Project

Before you can begin a science project, you need to understand the term *science project*. Older students are familiar with report writing. Many types of reports are required at all grade levels, whether it is book reports, history reports, or term papers. Although a report might be required to accompany your science project, it is not the focal point of a science project. The main idea of science comes from experimentation using a "scientific method." A scientific method uses a formal approach to scientific investigation. It is a step-by-step, logical thinking process that can be grouped into four sections:

1. The statement of the problem.

2. The hypothesis.

3. Experimentation and information gathering (results).

4. A conclusion based on the hypothesis.

When you first begin a science project, a statement of the problem must be made. A "problem" for scientists does not mean that something went wrong. A problem is something for which there is no good answer. For example, air pollution, aggressive behavior, crab grass, and obesity are problems. Any questions can be stated as a problem! Discuss your ideas for a science project with someone else, a friend, teacher, parent, or someone working in the field being investigated to give you a better understanding of your subject.

A hypothesis is an educated guess. It is educated because you use your life experiences to help you form an opinion. For example, your knowledge about trees—that they grow buds in the spring and drop their leaves in the autumn—helps you determine when seasons are changing. Your knowledge of dogs—that they growl when they feel threatened and wag their tail when they are amicable—can keep you from being bitten. These life experiences help you to form a specific hypothesis rather than a random one. Suppose you hypothesize, "If I add sugar to water and feed it to this plant, it will grow better." In order to prove this, you would first need a *control* plant, or a plant that is given only water—no sugar. Both plants would be given the identical amount of sunshine, water, temperature, and any other nonexperimental factor.

Assumptions

When you form a hypothesis, you must first define all of your assumptions. In the sample experiment I mentioned earlier, what does it mean that the plants will grow better? What is better assumed to be? Does it mean greener leaves, faster growing, bigger foliage, better tasting fruit, or more kernels per cob?

When growing plants from seeds, the assumption is made that all of the seeds are of equal quality. When several plants are used in an experiment, it is assumed that all of the plants are the same at the start of the project.

Before beginning your project, be sure to state all of your assumptions. If the results of any experiment are ever challenged, the challenge should be on the assumptions, not the procedures.

Sample Size

Sample size refers to the number of items in a test. The larger the sample size, the more significant the results. Using only two plants to test the sugar theory mentioned earlier would not yield a lot of confidence in the results. Maybe one plant grew better than the other just because some plants grow better than others!

The results of your statistical data becomes more meaningful when you sample a larger group of items in the experiment. This is because individual differences are less important (as the group size increases).

Measurements

Making accurate measurements is a must. The experimenter must report the truth and not let bias (his or her feelings) affect his measurements. As we mentioned earlier, the reason science progresses is because people do not have to rediscover well-known scientific principles with each new generation, or reinvent the wheel, so to speak. Science knowledge builds on what people have proven before us.

Consequently, it is important to record the results of your experiments. Keep accurate records of your controls, procedures, and recordkeeping. As you gather information, the results could lead to further investigation. Perhaps doing the experiment brought up more questions that need to be answered.

Conclusions

The conclusion of your science project must be related to your hypothesis. Was the hypothesis correct or incorrect? Perhaps it was correct in one aspect but not in another. In the sugar example we used earlier, adding sugar to the water might have helped, but only to a point. For example, the human body can use a certain amount of sugar for energy, but too much could cause obesity.

There is no failure in a science experiment. The hypothesis might be proven wrong, but you've still learned about something. Many experiments prove to be of seemingly no value, except that someone reading the results doesn't waste time repeating the experiment—and that is valuable. This is another good reason why it is important to thoroughly report results. Mankind's knowledge builds on past successes *and* failures.

Collections, Demonstrations, and Models

Competitive science fairs usually require experimentation. Collections and models by themselves are not experiments, although they can be turned into experiments. A collection is gathered data.

Suppose you have a collection of shells you assembled from along the eastern seaboard of the United States. The structure and composition of shells from the south could be compared to those found in the north. Then the collection becomes more experimental. Similarly, an insect collection can deal with insect physiology or comparative anatomy. A rock and mineral collection might indicate a greater supply of one type of rock over another because of the geology of the area from which they were collected. Leaves could be gathered from trees to survey the available species of trees in your area.

Often, science fair projects can be better served by demonstrations or models. These help others understand the scientific concepts you discovered during your project. For example, a steam engine dramatically shows how heat is converted to steam and steam is converted into mechanical energy. Seeing it happen can often have a greater impact than merely talking about it.

Although it is important to put some thought into how you want to present your data, remember that this is not the heart of the science fair project, but the scientific experimentation. You will want to discuss collections, models, and demonstrations with your teacher.

Choosing a Topic

Select a topic that interests you or arouses your curiosity. To get some ideas on a contemporary topic, just look through a newspaper: dolphins washing up on the beach, the effect of the ozone layer on plants, stream erosion, conservation, endangered species, oil spills, etc.

Safety Precautions

You must always place safety first when doing a science project. For example, using voltages higher than what is found in batteries, has the potential for electrical shock. Poisons, acids, and caustics must be carefully monitored by an adult. Temperature extremes, both hot and cold, can cause harm to objects and animals. Be careful of sharp objects or materials that can shatter such as glass. Nothing in chemistry should require tasting! Combinations of chemicals could produce toxic materials so take safety precautions. Some safety precautions include safety goggles, aprons, heat gloves, rubber gloves for caustics and acids, vented hoods, well ventilated areas, and adult supervision. You also need to give special consideration if a project is to be left unattended and accessible by the public.

Keep all of these safety factors in mind before beginning an experiment. Start by evaluating the materials list to see which safety precautions you will need to take. Any of the projects in this book that require an adult to help you, have a special stop sign icon at the beginning of the experiment and are indicated in boldface type.

Ethical Considerations

Most science fairs have ethical rules and guidelines for the use of animals. Live animals, especially vertebrates, are given thoughtful consideration. An example would be using mice to run through a maze demonstrating learning or behavior.

Some science fairs will require you to present a note from a veterinarian or other professional that states that you were instructed in how to deal with the animal.

Science Fair Procedures

Generally, science fairs lack well-defined procedures. The criteria for evaluation can vary from school to school, area to area, and region to region. There are a few things to keep in mind, however, before science fair projects are well under way.

Some teachers might require a group of students to work on a project together, but groups can be difficult for a teacher to evaluate. Who did the most work? Also, most science fairs do not accept group projects.

Limitations on time, help, and money are important factors. The question of how much money is to be spent should be addressed by a science fair committee. When entering a project in a science fair, generally the more money spent on the display, the better the chance of winning. It isn't fair that one child might only have $1.87 to spend on a project because of limited family income while another might have $250. Unfortunately, at many science fairs, the packaging does influence the judging. An additional problem is that one student's parent might be a science teacher or a professional in one of the sciences and another student's parent is not able to help them or is unavailable.

Science Fair Judging

Because science fairs lack well-defined standards, we would like to propose some goals for students and teachers to consider when judging.

A truly good project is one that requires creative thinking and investigation by the student. Recordkeeping, logical sequence, presentation, and originality are also important points.

The thoroughness of a student's project reflects the background work that was done. If the student is present, a judge might orally quiz the experimenter to test whether the student sufficiently understands the project. This also helps eliminate the unfairness of one student who might have the help of a knowledgeable adult while another does not.

Logging all experiences, such as talking to someone knowledgeable in the subject matter or reading material on it, will show the amount of research put into the project.

Clarity of the problem, assumptions, procedures, observations, and conclusions are important judging criteria too. Instruct students to be specific. Points should be given for skill, technical ability, and workmanship, which are all necessary to a good project. Skills could include computation, laboratory work, observation, measurement, construction, etc.

Often, projects with flashier display boards do better, and there is no doubt that some value should be placed on dramatic presentation, but it should not carry the point weight of other criteria, such as originality. Graphs, tables, and other illustrations can be good visual aids to the interpretation of data and students should be encouraged to include them. Photographs are especially important for projects where it is impossible to set the project up indoors, such as a "fairy ring" of mushrooms in the forest.

If a short abstract or synopsis in logical sequence is required, it should include the purpose, assumptions, hypothesis, materials, procedures, and the conclusion.

Competition

Science projects must often compete with others, whether it is at the class level or at a science fair. Find out ahead of time what the rules are for the competition. Check to see if there is a limit on size. Is an accompanying research paper required? Will it have to be orally defended? Will the exhibit have to be left unattended overnight. Leaving a $3,000 computer unattended overnight would be a big risk.

Find out what category has the greatest competition. You might be up against less competition by placing your project in another category. If it is a "crossover" project, you might want to place it in the category that has fewer entries. For example, a project dealing with chloroplasts could be classified as botany or chemistry. A project dealing with the wavelength of light hitting a plant could also be botany or physics.

Finally, we hope you get a good feeling of accomplishment as you delve into the fascinating world of botany, and that your first experience with science won't be your last.

2
New Plants from Old

Growing seeds is an excellent project for all ages. A seed has enough stored energy in it to grow a stem, push it through the soil, then form a leaf. Indeed, it is not just good enough for the stem to break through the soil surface, a leaf and root must form in order to absorb additional energy from sunlight, water, and nutrients from the soil. If a seed is outdoors and it takes too long to germinate, it could miss the growing season.

Seeds are very important to mankind. Essentially, every type of food we eat has its origin in some form of plant. The seed is the conclusion of a plant's life cycle (not that there are some plants that do not have seeds). It ensures continued growth of the species.

Continuation of a species is called reproduction. There are two principle types of reproduction: sexual and asexual. Asexual is a form of reproduction that does not use special reproductive organs. The vegetative parts of an existing plant (roots, stems, leaves) are capable of making new plants by vegetative propagation. In complex plants, asexual reproduction includes rhizomes, tubers, corms, and bulbs. These are naturally occurring. Artificial means are by cutting, grafting, and budding. Seedless grapes are grafted from an original plant, which occurred by accident.

Sexual reproduction is the fusion of the nuclei of specialized cells to produce a zygote. The zygote is the new organism.

PROJECT 2-1
Which Side Is Up
Adult Supervision Required

Overview

In nature, seeds are planted wherever they fall or travel. Some are buried or carried underground by animals. Others might go through the digestive tract for animals or birds then expelled through waste unopened. Farmers might also scatter seeds without regard for positioning. For seeds that are not round, will it matter whether they are planted horizontally or vertically? Is there an upside down where seeds are concerned?

Materials

- bean seeds (or other elongated seeds)
- 3, two-liter soda bottles
- potting soil
- 3 or 4 dark pieces of paper
- tape
- ruler
- marking pen
- note pad
- scissors

Procedure

Carefully cut the three, two-liter plastic soda bottles in half. Discard the top portion. Fill each container with soil. Determine that the light area on the seeds will be identified as "up." Plant three seeds near the wall of each container (as shown in Fig. 2-1). In one container, position them vertically. In another, place them horizontally, and in the last bottle, plant them diagonally. Three seeds are used in each container in case some seeds do not germinate. Plant all of the seeds at the same depth, covering the seeds with two inches of soil. Wrap a piece of dark paper securely around each bottle to allow the seeds to germinate in the dark. Place pieces of tape on the outside of the bottles and label the planting position of the seeds in each bottle. Keep the seeds moist without flooding them. Store them in a dark, warm, undisturbed location.

Form a hypothesis. For example, hypothesize that one position will grow better than the others. Observe the seeds each day. Keep an observation log such as the one suggested in Fig. 2-2. Open the

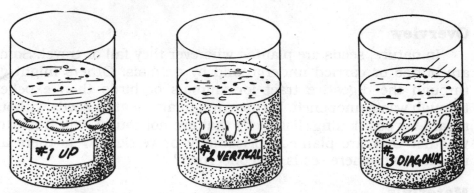

Fig. 2-1. *Plant three seeds near the wall of each container. Lay seeds horizontally in container #1, vertically in container #2, and diagonally in container #3.*

Date	Bottle #1		Bottle #2		Bottle #3
	up	down	diagonal up	diagonal down	vertical

Fig. 2-2. *Sample log for recording data for project* Which Side Is Up.

dark paper each day at the same time. Observe and record your observations by date. Measure any growth of stems or roots. Has the seed turned? Does its position hurt or help in its growth? Was your hypothesis correct?

Going Further

1. Will increased temperature help vertical seeds grow?

2. Will your results be true for carrots, acorns, corn, sunflowers, and other seeds?

PROJECT 2-2
Three Meals a Day

Overview

In some climates, rain occurs mostly at night (such as on smaller islands). In other areas, there is a rainy season with continuous rain for several weeks. Another form of plant watering would be dew from temperature changes between night and morning. Will watering seeds at different times of the day show any difference in growth? Growth will include the combined measurement of root and stem.

Materials

- 4 containers (3" to 4" in diameter)
- potting soil
- ruler
- notebook
- tape
- marking pen
- 32 green bean seeds

Procedure

Fill each of the four containers half full with potting soil. Place eight seeds near the sides in each container. Lightly cover the seeds with one inch of potting soil. Try to prepare all four containers in exactly the same way. Because this experiment tests watering practice, all other factors must be controlled. Be sure to label Jar #1 *3X* meaning three times a day, Jar #2 *Breakfast*, Jar #3 *Lunch*, and Jar #4, *Dinner*. Each container will receive six ounces of water for the first day, then three ounces per day thereafter. Water the containers using the following schedule.

JAR #1			JAR #2		
7 AM	1st day	2 oz	7 AM	1st day	6 oz
4 PM	1st day	2 oz	7 AM	2nd day	3 oz
8 PM	1st day	2 oz	7 AM	3rd day	3 oz
7 AM	2nd day	1 oz	(the pattern continues)		
4 PM	2nd day	1 oz			
8 PM	2nd day	1 oz			
7 AM	3rd day	1 oz			
4 PM	3rd day	1 oz			
8 PM	3rd day	1 oz			
(the pattern continues)					

JAR #3   JAR #4

4 PM   1st day   6 oz   8 PM   1st day   6 oz
4 PM   2nd day   3 oz   8 PM   2nd day   3 oz
4 PM   3rd day   3 oz   8 PM   3rd day   3 oz
(the pattern continues)   (the pattern continues)

Use the chart shown in Fig. 2-3 to record your observations.

Going Further

1. Cut the entire watering volume to a point where the roots are slightly deprived of water, watering them every four days.

Date	Jar # 1 3 X day	Jar # 2 breakfast	Jar # 3 lunch	Jar # 4 dinner

Fig. 2-3. *Sample log for recording data for project* Three Meals A Day.

PROJECT 2-3
Nighttime Grower

Overview

All growing organisms require rest. Do germinating seeds rest? If so, do they rest at night or during the day? Resting periods would be indicated by little or no growth in either the stem or the root. Are there periods when only the stem grows or when only the root grows? Form a hypothesis that seeds have a resting time.

Materials

- 8 green bean seeds
- potting soil
- clear plastic containers with drain holes in the bottom (two-liter soda bottle with holes punched in the bottom)
- ruler
- masking tape
- marking pen
- dark construction paper

Procedure

Fill the containers half full with potting soil. Place four strips of masking tape vertically at equal distances on one of the plastic containers as shown in Fig. 2-4. One container will be the control seeds. Plant seeds at equal depths, one on each side of each strip of masking tape. Draw a line on the tape to indicate the seed position. Also on the tape, place a number from one to eight, giving each seed an identifying number to track its progress. Seeds should be planted against the outside of the container so their root growth can be viewed and measured.

Wrap dark construction paper around the bottle to keep the seeds in darkness. Place the bottle in a warm place (70 degrees Fahrenheit) but out of direct sunlight. Water equally (about four ounces) daily. Remove the construction paper only long enough to observe what is going on with the roots of each plant. Use the observation log in Fig. 2-5 to record progress. Conclude whether your hypothesis was correct.

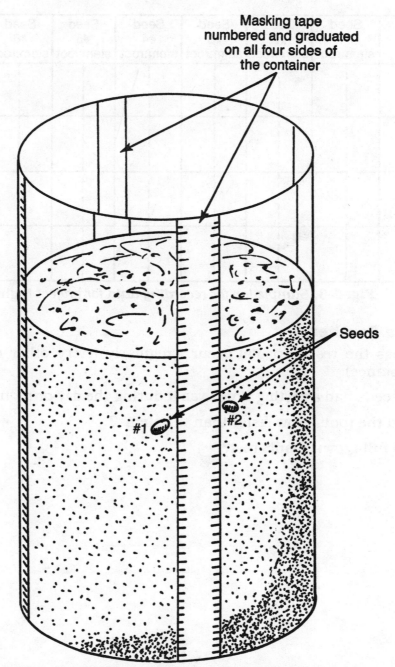

Fig. 2-4. *Place four vertical strips of masking tape at equal spaces on all four sides of the container.*

Date	Seed #1 stem:root	Seed #2 stem:root	Seed #3 stem:root	Seed #4 stem:root	Seed #5 stem:root	Seed #6 stem:root	Seed #7 stem:root	Seed #8 stem:root

Fig. 2-5. *Sample log for recording data for project* Nighttime Grower.

Going Further

1. Does the rest period(s) occur irregularly (every other day for instance).

2. If seeds had a resting time, was it during the day or night?

3. Did the roots grow faster than the stems?

4. Do full-grown plants rest?

PROJECT 2-4
Out Goes the Bad Air
Adult Supervision Required

Overview

Normally, we assume that plant material gives off oxygen and animals give off carbon dioxide (CO_2). This happens during photosynthesis. There might be a time when plant material gives off CO_2. Do germinating green bean seeds give off CO_2?

All matter takes up space, whether its a solid, liquid, or gas. Therefore, we can germinate seeds in a closed system and test for released carbon dioxide.

Materials

- thistle tube
- flask
- two-hole rubber stopper (that fits the flask neck)
- 1 glass tubing (about three inches long—can be straight or "elbow" shaped)
- 12 inches of clear plastic tubing (to fit over the glass tube)
- clear drinking glass (10 to 12 ounces)
- 2 dozen green bean seeds
- lime water
- tap water
- petroleum jelly
- safety goggles
- protective gloves

Procedure

Put on the safety goggles and the protective gloves before you begin the experiment, to protect against shattering glass. Insert the three-inch glass tube into the 12-inch plastic tube. Put the other end of the glass tube through one of the two holes in the rubber stopper. The tube should just barely stick out through the bottom of the stopper. Use caution when inserting glass tubing into the rubber stopper. Put a little petroleum jelly in the hole to aid in inserting the glass tubing. Insert the thistle tube into the other stopper hole with care. Check the depth of the tube when the stopper is put in place. The thistle tube should not be resting on the bottom but should be within two inches of it.

Fill the drinking glass with tap water. Put the two dozen bean seeds in the flask. Shake them to one side while inserting the stopper and thistle tube apparatus.

Put the plastic tubing into the drinking glass. Slowly pour water into the thistle tube. Pour enough so that the seeds are covered (about two or three inches). As you pour the water in, observe the air being forced out of the flask as air goes through the plastic tubing and bubbles in the drinking glass. Your system should now look like the setup shown in Fig. 2-6. Put it in a warm location but out of direct sunlight.

After three days, observe the clear tubing in the drinking water glass and the thistle tube. If any water has come up in either the clear plastic tubing or the thistle tube, then the volume of material inside the flask has decreased.

Remove the water from the drinking glass, and replace it with 2/3 full of lime water. The plastic tubing should go all of the way to the bottom of the glass.

Slowly pour water into the thistle tube. This will force gas out of the flask through the glass tube. Keep adding water until the level inside the flask reaches the tip of the rubber stopper.

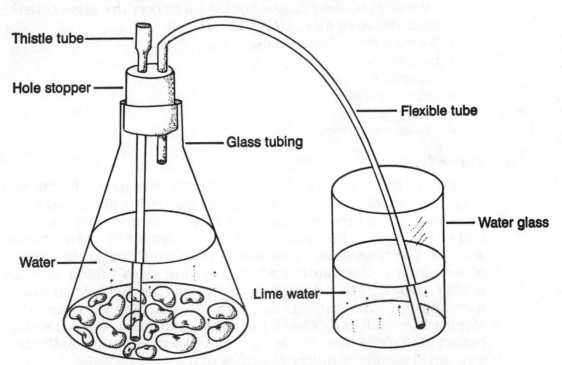

Fig. 2-6. *Construct this setup for detecting CO_2 coming from bean seeds.*

Bubbles should have come out through the lime water. If CO_2 is present, the lime water will turn a grayish, milky color.

Going Further

1. Is carbon dioxide heavier than water? Note when the lime water began turning milky. Was it when you first started adding water or not until the very end? This would indicate if CO_2 accumulated near the top or the bottom of the flask.

2. Is carbon dioxide heavier than air?

PROJECT 2-5
Mr. Potato Leg

Overview

Stems that grow underground store large amounts of food. These organs allow for early spring growth. The principle types of underground stems are rhizomes (iris), bulbs (tulips), tubers (potatoes), and corms (crocus). These plants can reproduce by "vegetative propagation." Vegetative propagation allows reproduction by using some part of the existing plant to grow an entire new plant. A potato grows underground and sends out stems that grow other plants above the ground. These plants produce food, which is stored in the ground as a potato. How much of the underground stem is required to produce a new plant?

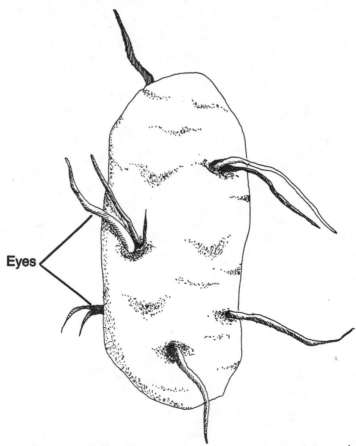

Fig. 2-7. Cut off the "eyes" of a potato and then plant them and try to reproduce potato plants by vegetative propagation.

Materials

- 3 irish potatoes
- 3 containers
- potting soil
- thermometer
- ruler

Procedure

Place three potatoes in a dark, dry place for several weeks. Allow eyes, or shoots to grow (Fig. 2-7). Cut off the "eyes." In one container, plant an entire shoot. In the second, plant three, one-inch sections. In the third, plant three half-inch sections taken from the middle of a shoot. Label the contents of each container. Cover with one inch of potting soil and water them. Keep them away from sunlight, equally moist, and at about 70 degrees Fahrenheit.

Continue growing them until the plants break through the top of the soil. Observe them to determine which grew fastest. Was there a dormancy period, that is, a resting time before growth could start? If so, can it be overcome in order to produce edible food more quickly?

Going Further

1. When plants have grown enough to be well out of the soil, separate them and continue to water them in equal amounts. Again, label containers and observe the total biomass (the entire structure) that appears above ground to determine if there are long-term effects due to the size of the shoot used in the beginning. Also, when the growing season is over, examine the potatoes that were produced.

2. What is the smallest amount of stem that will produce a plant?

PROJECT 2-6
Clip, Clip, Clip

Overview
Cuttings or clippings are an asexual form of reproduction. The stem part of some plants can be clipped, or cut from the parent plant and grow into an entire new plant. Horticulturists produce many plants in greenhouses using these methods. Roses, begonias, ivies, and geraniums are most often grown in this manner. Hypothesize which plants will grow from clippings.

Materials
- 8 to 10 small containers, jars, or test tubes
- 8 to 10 clippings of plants, including roses, begonias, ivy, geranium, African violet, several types of trees, and bushes
- masking tape or self adhesive labels

Procedure
Locate and clip eight to ten different plants. These plants can be found in your home, school, nearby forest or relative's or neighbor's gardens. Be sure to get permission to take pieces of plants from other yards, however. Clippings should include the stem with several healthy leaves. Label containers or test tubes and date them. Place the clippings in the containers with water then place them in sunlight similar to their natural surroundings. If the parent does not like direct sunlight, then do not put the clippings in direct sunlight. If the experiment works, roots will begin to develop from the bottom of the stem. Be sure the stem is always in contact with the water.

After a good root system has formed, transplant them to soil containers for additional growth to adulthood. Was your hypothesis correct?

Going Further
1. Attempt to grow new plants using only the leaf and the leaf stem (try an African Violet). Ask your local florist for several different leaves and stems.

2. Stress the clippings by depriving them of water for short daily periods. Will better roots form?

3
Photosynthesis

Have you ever picked up a piece of plywood that has been sitting on the ground and noticed that the patch of grass underneath has lost its green color? Without sunlight, chlorophyll departs from the leaves and photosynthesis cannot take place.

Photosynthesis is the process whereby green plants produce food. In food production, free oxygen is released. To do this, plants need CO_2, water, sunlight, chlorophyll, and trace amounts of minerals. Projects in photosynthesis can involve varying the amounts of any of these requirements, such as changing the temperature or introducing pollutants or trauma to the plant.

PROJECT 3-1
Wrap Up

Overview

This project could be titled *Carbon Dioxide Deprivation*. Green plants use carbon dioxide (CO_2) in a chemical process to produce simple foods. If CO_2 is not present, the process stops and the plants could starve. Some green plants might store a large quantity of food. Therefore, the amount of time to starvation might vary, but starvation will occur. Hypothesize which plants will die of carbon dioxide deprivation the soonest.

Materials

- 6 healthy plants
- 3 plastic bags
- 3 paper clips or clothespins

Procedure

Keep six plants in the same sunlit area, keeping all controls—temperature, water, movement, light, etc.—equal. Totally wrap three plants in plastic bags to prevent any carbon dioxide from going in and oxygen from escaping (see Fig. 3-1). Poke a hole in the top of the plastic to put water in. Except when giving the plant water, fold it over several times and use a paper clip or clothespin to keep the hole closed. Observe and note any and all changes.

Conclude whether your hypothesis was correct based on the results of your experiments.

Going Further

1. Using the CO_2 deprived plants setup, deprive all six plants of CO_2. Additionally, deprive three of the plants of water. Will the water make any difference? Will the plants need no water if they cannot have CO_2?

2. Use six plants that are CO_2 deprived. Place two in darkness without CO_2 or water, two in light with no CO_2 and no water, and the last two with only no CO_2.

To ensure that the least amount of CO_2 enters the bag, tape a watering tube with a funnel and stopper for watering. Use a support stick to hold the tubing, funnel, and bag upright. A small piece of wire or a garbage bag tie can be twisted around the watering tube to stop the water flow. Make sure the plastic tubing is in the soil. Also, keep water in the funnel even when the plant is not being watered and keep the wire twist tight to prevent CO_2 from entering the closed system.

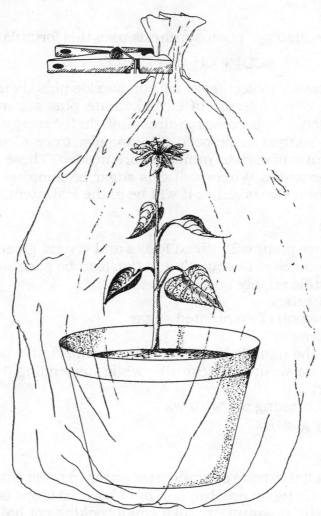

Fig. 3-1. *Wrap the plants in thin plastic to prevent the interchange of air.*

PROJECT 3-2
How Sweet It Is
Adult Supervision Required

Overview

The chemistry of photosynthesis uses this formula:

$$6CO_2 + 6H_2O \rightarrow C_6H_{12}O_6 + 6O_2$$

which means six molecules of carbon dioxide plus six molecules of water yield one molecule of carbohydrate plus six molecules of paired oxygen. The process requires sunlight for energy and chlorophyll as a catalyst (a helper). Additionally, trace elements (very small amounts of certain minerals) are needed. These are usually found in the water. Where will this sugar be found as a carbohydrate? Hypothesize whether it will be in the leaf, stem, or root.

Materials

- 1 house plant with green leaves and several green stems
- two ounces of Benedict's solution (can be purchased from a scientific supply house)
- 4 test tubes
- 1 teaspoon of granulated sugar
- eye dropper
- test tube hand-holder, ring stand setup, clothespin, or heat glove (to secure the test tube while suspending it in boiling water)
- small cooking pot with water
- safety goggles

Procedure

Put a half teaspoon of granulated sugar in a test tube half filled with water. Using an eye dropper, put about 20 drops of Benedict's solution in the sugar water. Fill a small cooking pot half way full of water. Place it on a stove and bring to a boil. (CAUTION: **have an adult with you when working around a stove.**) Also, wear safety goggles to protect against shattering glass. Shake the test tube and suspend it in the boiling water with a test tube hand-holder, clothespin, ring stand setup, or heat glove as shown in Fig. 3-2. Be

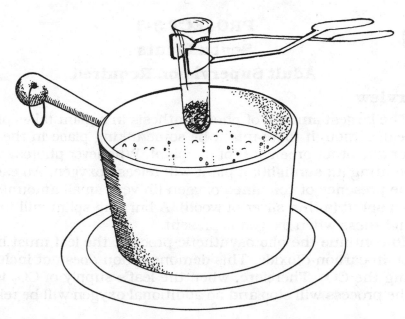

Fig. 3-2. *Use this "double boiler" arrangement for added safety.*

patient. When the solution heats up enough, you will observe a color change from the normal blue color of Benedict's solution. The color change can show an increasing sugar content:

green → yellow → orange

It is this color change that will determine whether sugar is present in the plant parts.

Next, test a piece of a leaf, stem, and root for sugar. This is done by crushing the leaf, stem, or roots into small pieces. Place the plant parts in a test tube half filled with water. Add 20 drops of Benedict's solution and place in a boiling pot. Observe any color changes and record the results.

Conclude whether your hypothesis was correct based on the results of your experiments.

Going Further

1. Using a healthy plant with several stems and many leaves, examine for sugar in the stem, leaf, and root parts during the late afternoon on a sunny day. Perform the same tests after 24 or more hours of artificially created darkness. Record your results and compare. Was sugar present in all parts in both tests? How will it compare to a normal plant?

2. Is there seasonal changes in sugar levels in various plant parts.

PROJECT 3-3
Scuba Plants
Adult Supervision Required

Overview

The largest amount of photosynthesis in a plant takes place in the leaf, although there might be some taking place in the stems and/or any other green part of the plant. Whenever photosynthesis is operating (in sunlight), a plant will release oxygen. An easy test for the presence of contained oxygen (in very small amounts) is to burn a splint (a thin sliver of wood). A burning splint will increase in brightness when oxygen is present.

To continue the photosynthetic process, the leaf must be able to obtain carbon dioxide. This demonstration does not include replacing the CO_2. Therefore, when the leaf's supply of CO_2 is used up, the process will stop and no additional oxygen will be released.

Materials

- 5 or 6 healthy leaves
- small funnel
- four-inch long wooden splint
- small aquarium tank, small tub, or large soup pot
- test tube (the funnel stem must be able to fit into it)
- masking tape and marker
- ruler
- protective gloves or tongs
- safety goggles

Procedure

Fill the tank, tub, or pot with water. Place the leaves topside up in the bottom and cover them with the funnel. Pay attention to which side is up when picking the leaves so you can determine which side is up when you place them in the large container. It is the top that must receive the sunlight. Be sure the top of the stem of the funnel is an inch or more below the surface of the water. Next, fill the test tube with water, being careful not to let air in. Place the test tube over the end of the funnel stem (as shown in Fig. 3-3). The entire apparatus must be placed in direct sunlight. Does anything happen? If the water is being replaced in the test tube, what is taking its place?

To test for the presence of oxygen, remove the test tube and carefully let out the remaining water. Hold the test tube with a glove

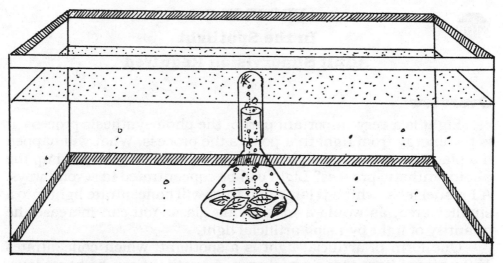

Fig. 3-3. *Place a test tube over an upside down funnel. Place leaves under the funnel. Fill the tank with water. Gases given off by the leaves will collect in the test tube.*

or tongs. Wear safety goggles to protect against shattering glass. Have an adult light the splint and after it is burning well, blow it out. Have them insert the glowing splint into the test tube. Be sure that the opening is not pointed at anyone. Was oxygen present? What did you observe?

The amount of oxygen can be quantified (measured) by marking the test tube before doing the experiment. Place a piece of tape from top to bottom along the side of the test tube. Mark off every quarter of an inch, putting numbers at each inch. Note the point on the test tube where the gas displaces the water. Later, fill the tube to the line with water and measure the volume of water, which will also be the volume of gas (oxygen).

Conclude whether your hypothesis was correct based on the results of your experiments.

Going Further

1. Using a test kit, measure for dissolved oxygen before and after burning splint wood. Is there more dissolved oxygen?

2. Is there a different quantity of oxygen if the leaves are picked early, at night, or in the late afternoon? You will need to make volume measurements.

3. Try different species of leaves. Use different parts of the plants. Try eloda or other aquatic plants.

PROJECT 3-4
In the Spotlight
Adult Supervision Required

Overview

Light is a very important part of the photosynthesis process. It is the energy from light that powers the process. What will happen if a plant receives more light? Will concentrated light speed up the photosynthetic process? Light can be concentrated in several ways. A Fresnel lens, which is large and thin, will concentrate light into a smaller area, as would a magnifying glass. You can increase the quantity of light by using artificial light.

One form of artificial light is a spotlight, which concentrates 150 watts of light into a small area. A spotlight can be hazardous, however, and should be used only with adult supervision. In an experiment of this type, the distance between the plant and the spotlight would be significant. As you move further away from the light source, the quantity of light arriving at the plant decreases greatly. Mathematically, the amount of light that reaches the subject is the inverse square of the distance (measured in lumens).

Materials

- mounted spotlight
- table (five feet longer or more)
- 3 healthy house plants
- 3 thermometers
- ruler

Procedure

Place a mounted spotlight at one end of a table. The light should be mounted high enough to shed light on the plants on the table but not to heat the table. Place three plants on the table. Position the first plant two feet from the lamp and a little to the right of the light (off center). Place the second plant three feet from the lamp and in the center, in direct line of the lamp. Place the third plant four feet from the lamp and to the left of the light. Each plant is a foot further away from the light source. Staggering the position of the plants prevents them from being shaded by one another. Figure 3-4 shows the setup.

Place a thermometer upright next to each plant to monitor the temperature at the plant's location. If the heat appears too exces-

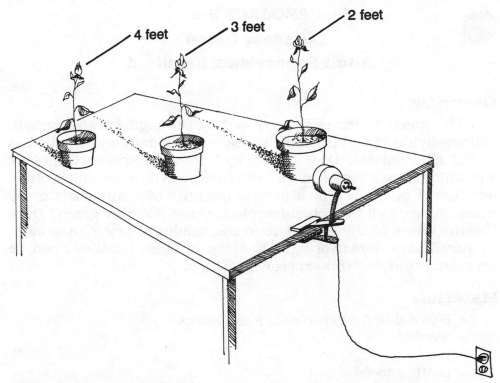

4 feet   3 feet   2 feet

Fig. 3-4. *Stagger the positioning of the plants so that one plant does not cast a shadow on another.*

sive, move all of the plants back further. Switch the light on for six hours a day. Observe the plants for several weeks.

Conclude whether your hypothesis was correct based on the results of your experiments.

Going Further

1. Establish an experimental process where one plant receives six hours of light using the spotlight, another plant receives eight hours of sunlight and a third plant receives 10 hours of sunlight. All of these plants should be placed in a row at equal distance from the light source.

2. Grow Lux light bulbs are designed specifically for plant growth. When you purchase one, the instructions will suggest a particular distance the lamp should be from plants. Regular fluorescent lamps can also be used for plant growth. Try setting up an area in a garage or cellar where your plants will not be disturbed and experiment with distances.

PROJECT 3-5
Greener Green
Adult Supervision Required

Overview

The green in leaves is produced by the pigment chlorophyll. Chlorophyll is contained in the palisade and spongy layers in bodies called chloroplasts. Does chlorophyll come in shades of green? Are chloroplasts larger in darker shades? Will more chlorophyll, whether it be caused by a greater quantity of chloroplasts or by more chlorophyll in each chloroplast, cause a darker green? Does the thickness of the leaf relate to the shades of green? Are more mature leaves darker or lighter? Many of these questions can be answered by doing this experiment.

Materials

- 6 to 8 different species of fresh leaves
- alcohol
- pot
- cutting tools
- paper and pen
- thin cardboard
- 6 to 8 test tubes
- test tube holder or protective glove
- safety goggles

Procedure

Arrange the leaves in order from lightest to darkest. Number the first leaf #1, the second #2, and so on. Place the number on a card or piece of paper. From each leaf, cut out an equal section, such as one square inch, for example. Make a card that is the same size. In this case, one square inch. Place it on the surface of each leaf. Continue cutting them out until you have one-inch squares on each of the numbers.

Next, set up the double boiler as shown in Fig. 3-5, with water in the pot and alcohol in the test tube. Use four ounces of alcohol in each test. CAUTION: **alcohol is highly flammable. Do not use a high flame to boil the water.** Wear safety goggles to protect against shattering glass. Have an adult help you boil the water in the pot. When the water begins to boil, turn down the heat to merely maintain the boiling condition. Use the least amount of heat

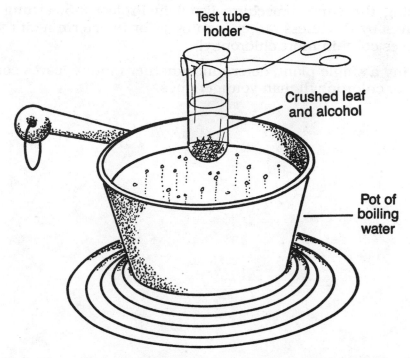

Fig. 3-5. *Use this "double boiler" arrangement for added safety.*

to keep the water boiling. Again, you must have an adult supervise you. Then, using a test tube holder or protective glove, place the test tube containing the leaf and alcohol into the boiling water. Bring the alcohol to a boil. Boil the alcohol for ten minutes. When it cools, set aside the test tube for later evaluation. Allow the alcohol to evaporate. This will, in some measure, allow you to quantify your chlorophyll results. Observe and record your data.

Complete the above procedure with each of the remaining test leaf pieces then conclude whether your hypothesis was correct based on the results of your experiments.

Going Further

1. Obtain a plant with many leaves. Remove ten leaves. Each day, test a different leaf for chlorophyll content. Observe whether or not chlorophyll is leaving the leaf as it gets older. You might want to do this on an every other day basis rather than every day.

2. Try doing these experiments using weight or mass rather than square area as a quantitative measurement.

3. Using the same procedure listed in Project 3-5, arrange the leaves by thickness rather than by color to determine if thicker leaves contain more chlorophyll.

4. Using a single plant, determine whether mature leaves contain more chlorophyll than younger ones.

PROJECT 3-6
Coniferous Versus Deciduous
Adult Supervision Required

STOP

Overview

Coniferous trees bear cones and are evergreen (green all year long). Deciduous trees have broad leaves that fall off each autumn. Hypothesize whether evergreen leaves (needles) have more or less chlorophyll per unit mass than deciduous trees.

Materials

- scale or balance beam (you can build one as shown in Fig. 3-6 if you need to)
- 3 sets each of evergreen needles (each set must be two to three dozen fresh needles and from different species of evergreen trees)
- 3 sets each of deciduous trees, each set must be two or three dozen leaves from different species of trees. We need chlorophyll extraction.
- alcohol
- double boiler pot
- 6 jars
- several small stones or weight sinkers
- scissors or sharp knife (take care using sharp tools)
- paper and pen

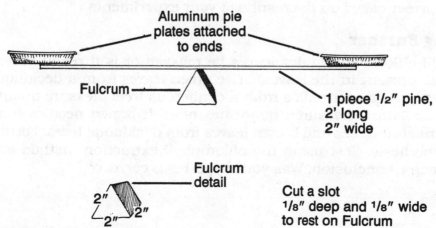

Aluminum pie plates attached to ends

Fulcrum

1 piece ½" pine, 2' long 2" wide

Fulcrum detail

2" 2" 2" 2"

Cut a slot ⅛" deep and ⅛" wide to rest on Fulcrum

Fig. 3-6. *Build a homemade balance beam if an accurate scale is not available.*

Procedure

Carefully cut away the lower one quarter of the needles and the leaves that were attached to the tree. You don't want to measure parts of the leaves that would not contain chlorophyll. Using the balance beam and the stones or sinkers, begin measuring the quantity of what you believe to be the lightest material. When you have measured that quantity, set the leaf material aside. Identify it as number one. All other measurements must be of the same quantity of weight. When you finish measuring the six groups, they will all weigh the same amount. Identify by numbers which species of tree each group is.

Next, using the chlorophyll extraction method, you will extract the chlorophyll from each group of leaves. Set up the double boiler with water in the lower pot and alcohol in the upper pot. Use approximately four ounces of alcohol in each test. **CAUTION: alcohol is highly flammable. Do not use a high flame to boil the water.** With an adult's supervision, boil the water in the lower pot. When the water begins to boil, turn down the heat to merely maintain the boiling condition. Use the least amount of heat to keep the water boiling. You must have an adult help you with this. Place the top pot containing the top part and the leaves over the boiling water. Bring the alcohol to a boil. Boil the alcohol for 10 minutes. When it cools, remove all of the material from the top pot and place it in a small jar.

Do this for each group and place each in separate jars. Allow the alcohol to evaporate, then examine the contents of the jars. Record your observations, then conclude whether your hypothesis was correct based on the results of your experiments.

Going Further

1. Will chlorophyll in dry leaves be masked or is it really absent (not present in the leaves)? Use green leaves from a deciduous tree and green needles from a coniferous tree. Measure quantities against measured quantities of each brown needles from coniferous trees and brown leaves from deciduous trees. Form a hypothesis. Test using the chlorophyll extraction method and reach a conclusion. Was your hypothesis correct?

PROJECT 3-7
No Smoking Area
Adult Supervision Required

Overview

In order to get carbon dioxide, plants breathe through the sto-mata on the underside of the leaves. Some plants that are near highways or in areas where air pollution is severe, suffer greatly. An example of that would be some of the large stands of trees in New England that are suffering because of industrial pollution from other areas. It has even been suggested that the increase in global pollution affects all trees.

Smoke also affects plants. One area where smoke affects plants would be in a contained area such as a restaurant. There are des-ignated areas where smoking is permitted and designated areas where smoking is prohibited. Admittedly, there may be exhaust fans and methods for clearing the smoke out of the air, but still, some plants might indeed be more smoke tolerant than others. Hypothesize they can be identified.

Materials

- 3 thin plastic bags
- 3 different species of healthy house plants (two of each species)
- adult smoker

Procedure

Hypothesize that one plant of the four will survive better than the others in the presence of smoke from a cigarette, pipe, or cigar. You might also hypothesize that one will do more poorly than the others.

Place a plastic bag over each plant and have an adult blow smoke into the bag. This must be done with three of the six plants. They should be placed in sunlight, and have the same soil struc-ture, watering schedule, and temperature. All non-test factors must be maintained. The control plants will be the ones that are main-tained without exposure to smoke. The plants that receive smoke must be covered for only an hour or two a day. In each case, fill the plant bag with smoke. At the end of an hour or two, remove the bag to allow the plant to get its carbon dioxide. Carbon monoxide is not recommended as a test pollutant. It comes from the exhaust of a car

Date	Plant Species 1		Plant Species 2		Plant Species 3	
	test plant	control plant	test plant	control plant	test plant	control plant

Fig. 3-7. *Sample log for recording data for project* No Smoking Area.

and is poisonous. It is odorless and tasteless, and therefore is too hazardous for our use.

Maintain a chart, such as the one shown in Fig. 3-7, to record your observations as you proceed through the experiment. Be sure to water the plants equally. When you have gathered all of your data, conclude from the results of your experiment whether your hypothesis was correct.

Going Further

1. Perhaps you could examine plants that are near heavily traveled roads because these have been subjected to carbon monoxide. Be sure to do this with adult supervision. Highways are not only hazardous to plants but also to pedestrians!

    Compare the plants growing along the highway with those of the same species growing in a backyard or an area removed from the highway and carbon monoxide.

2. Lichens, which are fungus and algae, symbiotic plants (helping each other) are very susceptible to airborne pollutants. Often, they are used to gauge air pollution.

4

Hydroponics

There are many reasons for growing our own plants and vegetables, but many people dislike the back-breaking toil required to maintain an outdoor garden. The smell of fertilizer, the biting of bugs, and the hot summer heat can put a damper on the joys of gardening. Plants can be grown more comfortably indoors using a technique called hydroponics. Some plants are naturally hydroponic, such as dune grasses that grow on the beach.

Many plants that are traditionally grown in the ground (geoponics) can grow without soil by feeding them with a nutrient liquid. The amount of available land to produce food is decreasing as the population increases. In Japan, for example, seaweed is used as food. Consequently, growing plants in a soilless culture is of great importance.

Dr. William Gericke, a professor at the University of California, grew a tomato plant 25 feet high in 1930 using a nutrient solution. Dr. Gericke discovered the exact proportion of mineral nutrients that was required for growing tomato fruit. He is credited with the coining of the term "hydroponics."

Advantages of Hydroponics

The advantages of hydroponics over traditional soil growing are many. Often, fruits and vegetables grown hydroponically have improved freshness and higher nutritional value. They can also be grown cheaper. Hydroponics is also environmentally sound. There is little wasted water or solution because plants are container-grown (water conservation). Pesticides are unnecessary. Because plants are given all of the nutrients they need, root systems are often less extensive than if the plant were in the ground where roots would have to grow long and search for food. This means that only minimum space is needed and more plants can be grown hydroponically in a smaller area. Indoor growing minimizes the need for chemical pest control, especially large animals such as rabbits. Temperature can also be controlled indoors. We can use artificial light. Crops can be grown all year round, and frost need not be a concern. A great advantage to indoor hydroponic growing is that it does not require back-breaking work. Anyone with a handicap that makes it difficult for them to work on the ground can set up a garden on a bench or table top. Finally, we can better control root rot, which occurs if soil remains too moist.

The Need for Hydroponics

Hydroponically grown food is well suited to desert regions or any area where water is scarce because water and nutrients are conserved.

Hydroponics has a special relevance in the space age. In the future, space stations, moon bases, and long-term vehicles will need to grow their own food and soil might not be available. Soil is too heavy to carry into space. Sunlight producing energy will not pose a problem, but space stations or vehicles will essentially be like separate planets. They might gather hydrogen in outer space, but they will not be able to obtain any additional oxygen. Therefore, any water or waste products of water must be reused. Soil quantity would be at a premium. Whatever was initially taken with them would be all that would be available.

Checking Your Water

The water that is used to grow plants hydroponically must be checked for pH, that is acidity (sourness) or alkalinity (sweetness). The term pH means potential hydrogen. It is measured on a scale from 1 to 14, with 7 being neutral, 1 being acid and 14 being alkaline (see the graph in Fig. 4-1). There is a factor of 10 between each value on the scale. For example, a pH of 5 is 10 times more acidic than a pH of 6, and a pH of 4 is 100 times more acidic than pH 6.

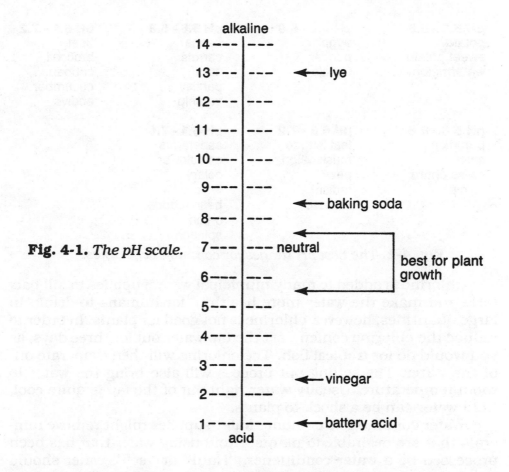

Fig. 4-1. *The pH scale.*

The pH should not be too low or too high, otherwise any nutrients in the solution are locked up and are unavailable to the plant. A very desirable pH for hydroponics would be between 5.5 and 6.5. The chart in Fig. 4-2 shows the best pH ranges for many popular vegetables. Measurements can be made very easily and very inexpensively with litmus paper (pH paper). Litmus paper and other test kits for checking the pH of water are available through many scientific supply houses, some of which are listed in the Resources list. Swimming pool test kits can be used, although they usually do not have a wide range and your water might read off the scale. If you need to change the pH of your water, Eco Enterprises and other hydroponic supply firms listed in the Resources list sell chemicals to add to your water to bring it into the pH range you need. Also, you can add potash to water if it is too acidic, or add sulfuric acid if it is too alkaline. Extreme caution should be exercised when dealing with sulfuric acid, however. It is highly caustic and can burn skin. Have an adult dilute some prior to use.

pH 5.0 - 5.6	pH 5.2 - 6.0	pH 5.6 - 6.8	pH 6.0 - 7.2
potato	eggplant	beans	beet
sweet potato	pepper	carrots	broccoli
watermelon	tomato	corn	cabbage
		parsley	cucumber
		parsnip	endive

pH 5.6 - 6.8	pH 6.0 - 7.2	pH 6.4 - 7.6
pumpkin	leaf lettuce	asparagus
salsify	muskmelon	cauliflower
swiss chard	peas	celery
turnip	radish	leek
	rhubarb	head lettuce
		onion
		spinach

Fig. 4-2. *The best pH ranges for common vegetables.*

Chlorine is added to many municipal water supplies to kill bacteria and make the water more healthful for humans to drink. In large quantities, however, chlorine is not good for plants. In order to reduce the chlorine content, set the tap water out for three days, as you would do for tropical fish. The chlorine will then evaporate out of the water. The setting out process will also bring the water to room temperature. Usually water right out of the tap is quite cool. Cold water can be a shock to plants.

Water conditioners on home water supplies might remove minerals that are desirable to plants. Avoid using water that has been processed by a water conditioner. "Hard" or "soft" water should not make any appreciable difference to your plants. Hard water contains salts of magnesium and calcium, which is generally good for plants.

Watering plants in hydroponics is also feeding, and it must occur on a regular schedule or the plants will become weak. A good rule of thumb is to match watering to a plant's usage of nutrients. If there is a lot of sun, give it lots of solution. If there is little sun, give it little solution.

The water in the growing container should not entirely cover the roots. Plants must be allowed to breathe, and so must part of the root system (see Fig. 4-3). In terrestrial plants, nitrogen-fixing bacteria changes atmospheric or free nitrogen into a form that can be used by plants. In hydroponics, nitrogen-fixing bacteria are eliminated. Therefore, nitrogen is a very important added ingredient.

Normally, you will use water from your kitchen sink in your projects. You might want to experiment with rainwater. For the

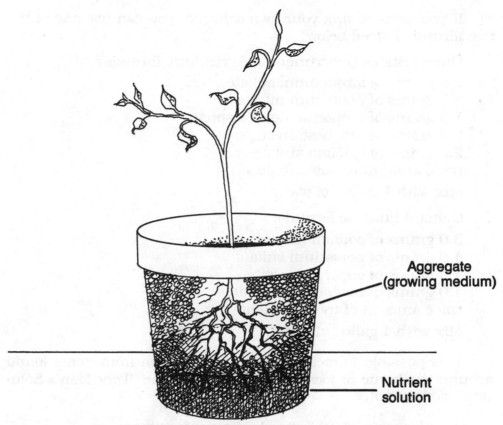

Fig. 4-3. *Plants need both moisture and aeration.*

most part, rainwater is pure, but particulate matter could be in it if you live near a big city or industry and that would be undesirable.

Nutrient Solutions

Nutrient solutions are a mixture of water and mineral salt fertilizers that provide all of the nutrition that a plant would naturally get from rain and soil. Solutions must be made (or purchased) before hydroponic experiments can begin.

There are hundreds of formulas, some for specific plants, some for growing larger vegetables, some for growing brighter flowers. Several standard nutrient solutions are the United States Department of Agriculture's formula and a general purpose formula that has been well tested throughout the years. Ready-made powders that can be mixed with water are available inexpensively from a list of suppliers whose names and addresses are given in the Resources list at the back of the book.

If you want to mix your own solution, you can use one of the two formulas listed below.

United States Department of Agriculture formula:

0.5 grams of ammonium sulfate
3.3 grams of potassium nitrate
1.5 grams of monocalcium phosphate
2.2 grams of magnesium sulfate
2.5 grams of calcium sulfate
trace amount of iron sulfate
Mix with 1 gallon of water

General Purpose formula:

3.0 grams of sodium nitrate
1.0 grams of potassium sulfate
1.3 grams of superphosphate
1.0 grams of magnesium sulfate
trace amount of trace elements
Mix with 1 gallon of water

It is possible to create a workable solution from items found around the home or local grocery market. The "Poor Man's Solution" consists of:

1 tablespoon	5-10-5 standard plant fertilizer
1 teaspoon	Epsom salts
1 teaspoon	washing ammonia

Mix with a gallon of water. The contents of the "Grocery Store Solution" are:

1 teaspoon	baking soda
1 teaspoon	Epsom salts
1 tablespoon	saltpeter
1 tablespoon	washing ammonia

It too should be mixed with one gallon of water. In these formulas, Epsom salts provide magnesium sulphate and saltpeter provides sodium nitrate.

If you choose to make your solution using one of the first two formulas, we recommend purchasing chemicals that are *agriculture grade* rather than *laboratory grade*. These are less expensive and might also contain trace elements in the form of impurities, but these are desirable.

The chart in Fig. 4-4 shows most of the known elements used by plants and the functions they perform.

Is it possible to create a solution by leaching soil from the ground? One of the experiments in this chapter investigates leaching.

Elements	Source and Functions
Carbon	Gets carbon from CO_2 in the air through leaf stomata. Carbon, oxygen, and hydrogen manufacture carbohydrates (food for the plant).
Oxygen	Gets through stomata (atmosphere) and through roots (water).
Nitrogen	Required in production of leaves and stem growth—stimulates green growth. Source: Potassium nitrate, sodium nitrate, and calcium nitrate {which also provides potassium, sodium (not needed by plants), and calcium, water (H_2O)}.
Phosphorous	Develops flower blooms and fruit, and good roots. Source: Ammonium phosphate (best source).
Potassium	Gives good strength and turger (woody stems), and pulp of fruit. Source: potassium sulfate. Common source: potash and saltpeter (saltpeter is potassium nitrate).
Calcium	Root growth. Aids in absorption of potassium. Gives structural rigidity. Source: calcium sulphate.
Magnesium	Distributes phosphorous throughout plant. Aids in chlorophyll production. Source: magnesium sulphate, magnesium nitrate. Common source: Epsom salts (mag. sulphate)

Fig. 4-4. *Common elements used by plants and the functions they are known to perform.*

Fig. 4-4. *Continues.*

Sulphur	Used in energy production (protein formation).
Iron	Used in chlorophyll production. Source: ferrous sulphate, feric chloride.
Manganese	Assists absorption of nitrogen. Source: manganese sulphate, manganese chloride.
Zinc	Used in energy transference process.
Boron	Makes cell walls permeable to sugars. Source: boric acid, trace amounts found in copper sulphate and zinc sulphate. Common source: Borax.
Copper	Used in chlorophyll production.
Iodine	Intensifies leaves' green color.
Chlorine	Controls water intake and transpiration.
Molybdenum	Used in process of assimilation.
Cobalt	Aids in formation of vitamin B-12 and DNA synthesis.

Growing Mediums

When plants are grown in a 100 percent nutrient solution, this special method of hydroponics is sometimes referred to as aquaponics. This technique requires some sort of support for the plant. Usually, it is easier to grow plants in some type of growing medium that can help support the plant's root system. As long as the growing medium, sometimes referred to as an aggregate, does not add any nutrients to the plant, the method is considered to be hydroponic. Examples of material that can be used as "soilless" growing mediums are: sand, gravel, LECA, or light expanded clay aggregate (see Fig. 4-5), small stones, colored gravel (sold in pet shops for aquariums), cinders, volcanic lava, charcoal, sawdust, vermiculite, and perlite.

Vermiculite is a natural occurring mineral containing millions of tiny cells. These cells store air and water. It does decompose over time, but does not affect soil pH and has no food value for plants. Perlite is light, rocklike porous pebbles. Both vermiculite and perlite can be purchased at garden and hardware stores.

Each medium has its advantages and disadvantages. Its purpose is to allow moisture and oxygen to get to the plant's roots, and also to physically support the plant. In nature, earthworms crawl through the ground to aerate the soil. You can use most any inert objects as a growing medium. Lettuce has been grown on a sheet of styrofoam, but this is not the best medium. Sometimes, the best mediums are combinations. A mixture of equal parts of vermiculite, perlite, and peat moss is often used. Even soil in which all the nutrients have been used up can be considered for your projects.

Experiments in hydroponics can center around growing plants in 100 percent solution or in a soil-like material that has no nutrient or food value for the plant.

Fig. 4-5. LECA, or light expanded clay aggregate, is a commonly used growing medium for hydroponics.

Problems

As you prepare for your experiments, keep in mind that nutrient solutions must be changed frequently. This is to renew oxygen and minerals. Furthermore, as water evaporates, the solution can become more acidic.

The solution should not be in direct sunlight. If you are using a test tube to grow a clipping, or growing a seedling in a jar, cover the area where the solution would be exposed to light in order to reduce the growth of algae. If during your experiments, large quantities of green algae material are found in the container or on the root system, remove the plant. Rinse it thoroughly under running tap water. Completely clean the container or use a new container. Place the plant back into the container and add new nutrient solution. Algae growth is unattractive, smelly, and competes with the plant for nutrients.

It is important to keep a close watch on your plants for any signs of trouble. If trouble occurs, try to find out what is going wrong and make corrections quickly. When a child cries, he is trying to tell you something. You must determine the cause. Is he wet, tired, hungry? With plants, the leaves are your guide. The chart in Fig. 4-6 shows some symptoms and causes that can help you.

Plants will often lose some leaves when they are transplanted or moved from one location to another. This does not necessarily mean there is a problem. It is a normal adjustment while the plant gets acclimated. Keep watching for new shoots and leaves. Remove yellow leaves. Trim brown tips. This can be done with scissors and does not harm the plant.

The biggest problem in hydroponics is keeping the water level at an optimum level. If you do not tend to your plants for a few days, the water might be used and evaporation takes place, exposing too much of the root and dehydrating the plant.

Hydroponics can be done outside, but you must shield plants from strong winds and too much rainfall. Also, there are more high and low temperature extremes outside as well as an increased risk to diseases and pests.

When mixing hydroponic solutions, do not get carried away and put too much fertilizer in the water. If there are too many nutrients in the water, the plant actually loses water to the solution and dehydrates.

Keep plants away from hot stoves, fumes, gas ranges, and cigarette smoke. Occasionally spray a mist of water on all leaves to remove dust and particles that might clog the stomata.

While the best sunlight might come from a window, watch your plant to see if it dislikes the winter cold, which it might feel being close to a window at night.

Learn about the type of plant you are growing. Problems may arise because you are not growing the plant in the environment that it likes, and you might think your experiment is a failure. Some plants, such as lettuce, like cool growing temperatures. African violets, forget-me-nots, impatiens, and wax begonias like a lot of

Symptom	Causes
Yellow or pale leaves	Nitrogen deficiency Magnesium deficiency Sulfur deficiency
Purplish or reddish leaves	Phosphorous deficiency
Small leaves	Boron deficiency
Thin foliage	Zinc deficiency
Green veins on yellow leaves	Iron deficiency
White areas around veins in leaves	Oxygen deficiency
Wilting	Hydrogen deficiency
Poor growth	Nitrogen deficiency Water pH out of plant's range Insufficient aeration of roots Calcium deficiency Sulfur deficiency Manganese deficiency Chlorine deficiency
Poor resistance to diseases	Potassium deficiency
Small, thin skinned fruit	Potassium deficiency
Weak stalks	Potassium deficiency

Fig. 4-6. *Common symptoms and causes of plant problems.*

shade. Peas prefer full sun. Rotate ornamental plants to maintain an even shape if grown near a window.

In hydroponics, it is important to keep in mind the differences in plant species. Some species might be better adapted to growing hydroponically. A good example is lettuce. Lettuce is grown agriculturally indoors by hydroponics in a very large production situation. There is an operation in the southern United States that grows over 5 million heads of lettuce a year hydroponically. Generally, these crops are easiest to grow hydroponically: lettuce, dwarf tomatoes, strawberries, and cucumbers.

Containers

Beginning a hydroponic garden can require a little innovative thinking. A germination bed must not hinder the seed growth. The root system must grow down and the stems must grow up. Some types of seeds cannot have pressure on their sides or they will not germinate. They must be free to push open their shells.

A variety of growing containers can be used, anything from test tubes to wide mouth jars to aquarium tanks. An old sink, glazed earthenware vessels, metal buckets painted with asphalt, and troughs can be used. Each requires some thought as to how the plant is to be supported. Dr. Gericke's technique used large waterproof basins with wire grids to support the plant. The roots dangled down into the solution. A bedding of dried hay or peat moss covered the top to keep light out, moisture in, and to let air freely circulate. When choosing a growing container, keep these points in mind:

1. It must not be affected by acid nor alkaline.

2. It must not rust.

3. It must be waterproof.

4. It must not give off any toxic substances.

Are You Ready? Let's Grow!

Want to learn a new word or two? A hydroponic growing unit is called a *hydroponicum*. If you grow plants hydroponically, you are called a *hydroponicist*. Does that title make you feel important?

PROJECT 4-2
Wet or Dry

Overview

Some soils can hold more water and for longer periods of time than other soils. When dealing with the needs of plants, we must realize their need for moisture. Some plants deal with the need for moisture by having a large diameter root system. Other plants might have long tap roots that go straight down. All of this is conditional to the top layers of soil around the roots and how well that soil holds water as well as for how long. Some soils will hold more water than others. Some soils will hold water longer than others. We will compare four different types of soils and determine which ones hold more water and which ones hold water for the longest period of time.

Materials

- cheesecloth, about one yard wide by a yard long
- 4 containers, such as a five-pound coffee can or cut a third of the top off of a three-liter plastic soda bottle
- 4 different types of soil, such as potting soil, vermiculite, perlite, sand, backyard soil (vermiculite and perlite are available at hardware stores)
- 4 rubber bands
- clock or watch
- scissors
- paper, pen and transparent tape
- measuring cup

Procedure

Carefully cut the cheesecloth into four equal pieces. In the center of each piece, place a sample type of soil (medium). Suspend the medium and cheesecloth inside the top of the container so that the cheesecloth folds around the outside of the container and the medium is held completely within the cheesecloth (see Fig. 4-8). Use a rubber band to hold the cloth in place. Do this with each soil sample, then label the containers with the type of soil that is in them.

Pour a measured amount of water into the medium in one of the containers. Do the same with each container. We suggest pouring a cup or two of water in each, but not so much as to have the

PROJECT 4-1
Half Baked
Adult Supervision Required

Overview

Neighborhood soils contain many living organisms: insects, seeds, rhizomes, bacteria, and the like. In addition, there is material in the process of decomposition. Evaluating the soil with a hand lens will reveal this but microscopic evaluation will indicate the presence of many more interesting organisms and materials.

Heating soil to 400 degrees Fahrenheit for 15 to 20 minutes will effectively kill most of the living material. Although, there are bacteria that will not only survive at this temperature, but will reproduce and grow. One hypothesis can be that an unbaked container of soil from outdoors will produce plants that were initially unseen. The baked sample will not.

Materials

- 2 nine-inch aluminum pie plates
- 2 old dinner plates
- enough backyard soil to fill two, nine-inch pie plates 2" high
- use of an oven (CAUTION: **An adult should be present whenever you use an oven.**)
- pot holders

Procedure

Take some soil from around your house. Do not dig very deep. Ask your parents permission first. The surface soil should be relatively free of any visible plant growth. If it has a few pieces of grass or weeds growing in it, pull them out along with their roots and discard them.

Fill the two aluminum pie plates with the soil samples. Place one plate in an oven and have an adult help you bake it at 400 degrees for 15 to 20 minutes. Use the pot holders to remove the plate, then let cool.

Place both soil samples in equally warm, sunny windows (Fig. 4-7). To keep the possibility of any new airborne seeds and the like from falling into the soil samples, keep them indoors and away from open windows. If the pie plates you bought have small pin holes in the bottom of them, set an old dinner plate underneath them to keep water from running onto the floor when the soil is watered.

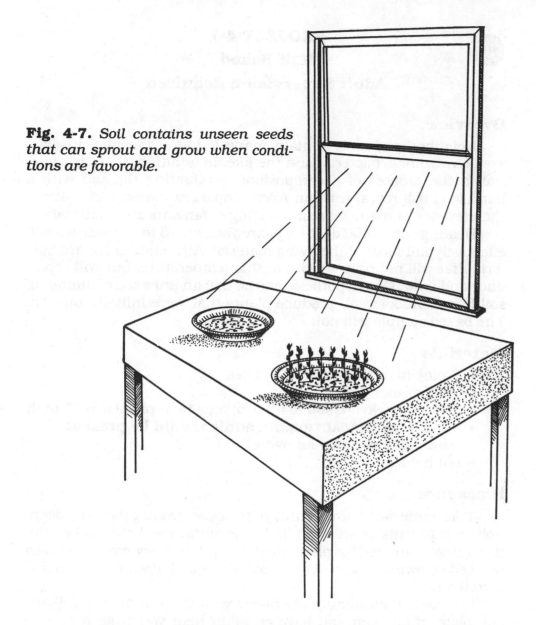

Fig. 4-7. *Soil contains unseen seeds that can sprout and grow when conditions are favorable.*

Water each sample, keeping them moist. You might feel a little foolish watering dirt, but after a period of time you might see some plants growing. Attempt to identify the types of plants that appear. Are the same types of plants growing in each pie pan? Is the quantity of total growing material the same?

Conclude whether your hypothesis was correct or not based on the results of your experiment.

Going Further

1. Try several neighborhood sites for soils. Do not dig up a public park, however, or you could be fined.

2. If possible, use forest soil. Compare soils from various depths. For example, one batch of soil could be taken from the surface to a depth of two inches. Another could be from two inches to four inches, and another from four to six.

3. Compare soils below different grass species.

4. Bake two pie tins full of soil at 400 degrees for 20 minutes. Place one outside on a deck or a porch, but not at ground level. Place the other inside the house in a sunny spot. Water both regularly. Did more grow outside than inside? If so, what caused the growth?

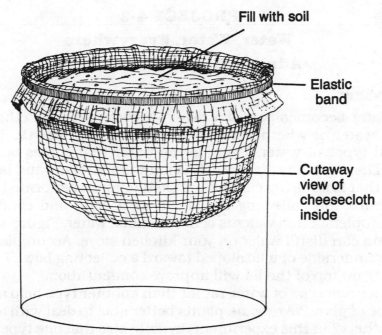

Fill with soil

Elastic band

Cutaway view of cheesecloth inside

Fig. 4-8. *Measuring the ability of soil to hold moisture.*

level of the accumulated water come up and touch the bottom of the cheesecloth. You want as much of the water to drain through as it can and not be in contact with the medium or the cheesecloth.

A criteria for this project is not only how much water drains through each soil type but also how long it takes to do so. If it takes a long time, but it drains almost completely through, then natural watering would have to occur with some frequency. However, if the medium remains moist for long periods of time and less water drains through, then the sample soil will remain wet longer and therefore, will be able to keep the roots of plants in contact with moisture.

Hypothesize which soil sample will remain wet the longest before you start your test. Be sure to keep good notes. Conclude whether your hypothesis was correct or not based on the results of your experiment.

Going Further

1. Using soils in your own area, dig holes of equal depth and size in several different areas. Pour equal amounts of water in each and measure the length of time it takes the water to drain out of the hole. This is called percolation.

PROJECT 4-3
Water, Water, Everywhere
Adult Supervision Required

Overview

Water becomes part of a plant's environment, whether it lives in the water or whether it receives water for its growth. There are several types of water. There is the water that comes out of your sink. There is rainwater, which is found in streams and lakes, and water that is made by distillation. Distillation is performed by creating steam and collecting the steam as it cools and condenses to form droplets. Such water is called distilled water. Figure 4-9 shows how you can distill water on your kitchen stove. Accumulate steam on the underside of a lid sloped toward a collecting bowl. Ice placed in a bag on top of the lid will improve condensation.

Does one type of water rather than another type help a particular type of plant? Are some plants better able to deal with all waters than others? In this experiment, hypothesize that one type of house plant will grow better than another, depending on the type of water it receives.

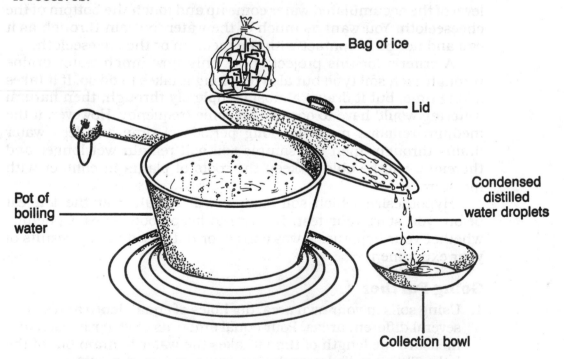

Fig. 4-9. *Distilled water can be made by condensing steam.*

Materials

- 4 clean two-liter plastic soda bottles (scrubbed clean, but without soap)
- 1,000 milliliters of water from a nearby lake or stream
- 1,000 milliliters of rainwater gathered from above the ground so no soil splashes into it
- 1,000 milliliters of tap water from your sink
- 1,000 milliliters of distilled water
- 4 equally healthy house plants
- measuring cup

Procedure

Gather 1,000 ml of each type of water. Identify one plant as receiving only lake water, one for rainwater, the third for tap water, and the last for distilled water. Using the house plants with all variables held equal (temperature, sunlight), water each of the identified plants the same quantity of water every four days (approximately 200 ml). Water should be at room temperature. Keep the water out of sunlight to reduce algae growth.

Set up a log for observations. The tap water is the control plant. The other plants are the test plants. After the last watering and several days wait, gather your last observations and conclude whether your hypothesis was correct.

Going Further

1. Check each type of water for pH. Determine by the pH which plant will be healthier.

2. Measure the waters for nutrient content: potassium, nitrates, and dissolved oxygen, using water test kits.

3. Evaluate microscopically for organisms found in the different waters. Suggest the hypothesis that the more organisms present in the water, the better the plant growth will be.

PROJECT 4-4
Don't Get Bogged Down

Overview

A bog contains slow or stagnant water. Sometimes, bogs form from a loop in a slow moving stream. The standing water produces high concentrations of tannic acid from trees. Therefore, the pH will be low, usually between 4 and 5. Bogs can be open, appearing as large grassy fields (Fig. 4-10), or they may be closed with cedar forming a canopy layer. Is bog soil rich in nutrients? Are clays present? Hypothesize what you will find in bog soil that cannot be found in forest soil.

Fig. 4-10. *Examining bog soil.*

Materials

- hand lens (magnifying glass)
- screen for sifting soil
- containers to carry and hold soil
- shovel for digging

Procedure

Remove a quantity (a bucket full) of soil from a bog. In another container, place a shovel full of forest soil. Screen each of the samples for large particles. Figure 4-11 shows some commercially available soil sieves, each having screens with various size openings.

Fig. 4-11. *Commercially available soil sieves, each with a screened bottom with different sized openings in the mesh.*

Evaluate and record your observations. Using a smaller screen, sift again to see what other particles might be present. Examine them with a hand lens. Attempt to identify what you find.

Did you hypothesize that the bog would have more decomposing or deteriorating material or less? Conclude whether your hypothesis was correct based on your observations.

Going Further

1. Test both soils for nitrogen content.

2. Weigh out an equal amount of both soils. Cook out all the moisture and bake the soils at 400 degrees Fahrenheit (you must have an adults supervision around an oven). If there are materials present that will burn, then the samples' weight will be reduced by the material that became ash. Weigh them again and calculate and compare the differences.

PROJECT 4-5
Irrigation Agitation

Overview

More oxygen is produced in the oceans through the photosynthetic process by algae than all of the terrestrial plants (plants grown in soil). The algae in the oceans are receiving all the nutrients and all of the necessary materials for life. People of different cultures set algae from the oceans. Algae is used in many products that we in the United States consume. Hypothesize whether it is possible to set up a saltwater environment and grow algae.

Materials

- aquarium, about 10 to 12 gallon capacity
- seawater
- algae living in seawater
- sunlit area
- ruler or scale
- container to carry seawater (gallon milk jug or three-liter soda bottle)
- adult help to transport seawater
- optional siphon to remove seawater from aquarium during changes

Procedure

Measure the mass of the algae. This can be done using a ruler to measure its size or a scale to measure it's weight. Fill the aquarium with seawater, and place the algae in it (Fig. 4-12). The nutrients and dissolved oxygen in the seawater will soon be used up by the algae. After two days, replace the seawater with "fresh," (room temperature) seawater. Replace the seawater every three days. Do this for five or six changings. Then measure the quantity of algae again. If you hypothesized in the beginning that the algae would survive and grow larger, then conclude whether your hypothesize was correct or not.

Going Further

1. Attempt to keep the algae alive by putting living saltwater animals into the solution to provide carbon dioxide. Add only enough solution to make up for evaporation.

2. Test at different temperatures. Maintain the aquarium at 65 degrees. Use an aquarium heater if necessary. Compare the growth at 65 degrees to that of 70 degrees, 75 degrees, and higher. In each case, measure the size or weight to determine the growth.

3. Use seawater near the shore and farther out away from shore. Attempt to determine whether the closer seawater has a greater ability for growing algae.

4. Evaporate seawater to gain the "salts" that it contains. Compare the volume of seawater to the quantity of salts that it contains. Can you maintain a saltwater environment using these salts that you have extracted to make a solution with fresh water or distilled water. Evaluate the pH of your solution before evaporation and again after the construction of your homemade seawater. Will there be a difference?

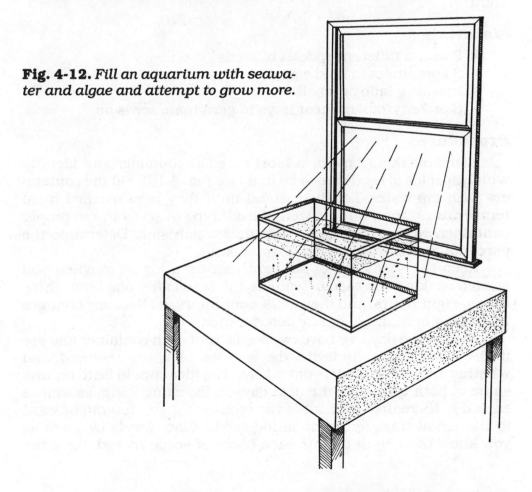

Fig. 4-12. *Fill an aquarium with seawater and algae and attempt to grow more.*

PROJECT 4-6
Underwater Swimmers

Overview

Seeds can be transported over great distances. In order to be able to grow once they find themselves in soil or in a moist environment, they must not have rotted. In order to break open the seed coat, however, they must be at least moist. What happens to seeds if they are left in water for a week? Do they change? Do they rot? What is the longest they can be left in water before they are no longer able to germinate? Your hypothesis could be that: some seeds will not germinate if soaked for more than two days; seeds will all sink after being in water for two days; seeds will germinate no matter how long they are in the water so long as they do not rot or deteriorate. Any of these hypothesis would work with this experiment.

Materials

- 3 dozen different species of seeds
- 3 containers to hold water
- masking tape or labels
- 6 or 7 styrofoam meat trays to germinate seeds on

Procedure

Place masking tape or a label on each container and identify which species of seeds are to go in it (see Fig. 4-13). Fill the containers with tap water. Let them stand until they have reached room temperature, then put a dozen of each type of seeds in the proper container. Note which seeds float and which sink. Determine the percentage of the seeds that float (or sink).

Keep the seeds out of sunlight. Set up a log as to when you started soaking the seeds. Evaluate the seeds after one hour, three hours, eight hours, and then at 24 hour intervals. Note any changes in floating or sinking, or any deterioration.

After three days, remove two seeds from each container and see if they germinate. Indicate the species of seeds removed and whether they were floaters or sinkers. The ideal would be to remove some of both types. On the next day, do the same thing, as well as each day thereafter until all of the seeds are gone. You might want to use small trays for germinating seeds. Place labels by them so you know the length of time each batch of seeds soaked. Keep the

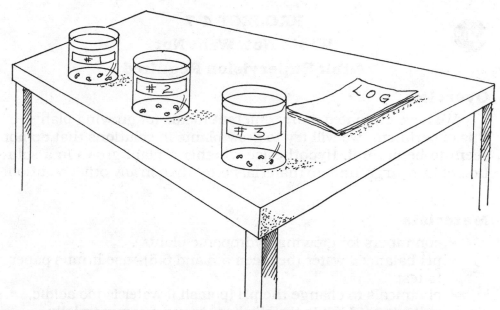

Fig. 4-13. *Seeds that can float for long periods of time stand a better chance of being transported greater distances from the parent plant by streams.*

germinating seeds moist, but not soaked. They won't germinate if they are not moist. Keep good records, then conclude whether your hypothesis was correct.

Going Further

1. Use other species of seeds. Determine which are more suitable for being transported by water over long periods of time.

2. Will some seeds remain viable (able to be germinated) no matter how long they are under water? You might want to make a longer experiment by keeping seeds in water for a longer period of time.

3. Will some seeds that are held down in the water (because they want to float) last longer than seeds that sink? Do floaters remain viable longer than sinkers if held under water?

PROJECT 4-7
Waste Not, Want Not
Adult Supervision Required

Overview

We have evaluated many different media for growing plants. In this experiment, we will try to grow plants in solutions that do not seem to be natural. Hypothesize whether a plant grows in a solution of its own ground-up material better than in any other solution.

Materials

- containers for growing hydroponic plants
- pH balanced water (between 5.5 and 6.5)—use litmus paper to test
- chemicals to change the pH (potash if water is too acidic, sulfuric acid if it is too alkaline, or use a commercially available "pH Up" or "pH Down" solution)—**DANGER: sulfuric acid can burn the skin. Wear safety goggles to protect your eyes and protective gloves to protect your hands.**
- four plants, a species of plant that grows quickly (an indoor house plant such as philodendron)
- blender of food processor
- hydroponic nutrient solution
- vermiculite, perlite, or some type of soilless growing medium

Procedure

Remove all of the soil from three healthy plants. Leave the fourth plant in its soil-growing medium (potting soil). Put one plant in a container to be grown hydroponically. Use a blender or food processor with pH balanced water to mulch the other two plants. Be sure the solution is very thin. Add a lot of water (see Fig. 4-14).

Use the pH balanced solution to water the soil plant. Use your homemade hydroponic solution for feeding the second plant. To improve the validity of the experiment, use several plants in each group. Cover the containers of the hydroponic plants to reduce the light hitting the solutions.

Measure the quantity and health of the plants (the quantity of leaves, their size) to later make a comparison for growth. Record their condition: wilting, green appearance, turgor (whether or not

Potting soil plant.
Feed with tap water.

Hydroponic plant in
vermiculite. Feed with
homemade solution.

Fig. 4-14. *Feed the plant a solution of ground up material of the same species of the plant.*

the plant is limp). Keep a daily record. Water the soil plant every two or three days with small amounts of water.

Run your experiment for several weeks, noting the plants' conditions each day. Record your results, then conclude whether your hypothesis was correct.

Going Further

1. Attempt to grow food-producing plants such as green beans (bush variety), carrots, and the like.

2. Try, using clippings from your grass, to fertilize a section of lawn. Grass clippings are in great abundance and should not be hard to come by.

3. Use vegetative waste material, such as the leaves from lettuce and the peelings from carrots, to produce a solution for indoor plants.

PROJECT 4-8
How Much Is Enough?

Overview

We have discussed the need for light in the photosynthetic process. Will hydroponic plants grow in very small quantities of light? Does light directly affect food growth? The answers to these questions would be very valuable knowledge in planning a space station where all energy must be used sparingly and wisely. Hypothesize whether or not the plants that receive the shortest period of light will be able to survive.

Materials

- artificial light source
- several hydroponically growing plants

Procedure

Set up your hydroponically growing plants under artificial lights. Give one plant one hour of light per day, another plant two hours of light per day, a third three hours, and a fourth one five hours.

Establish a log such as the one shown in Fig. 4-15 to record your observation. Run your experiment for several weeks, noting both the quantity of leaves, the total mass of the plant, and the overall health (color, turgor, and so on). All other variables such as heat and water must be controlled.

Date	1 Hour of light	2 Hours of light	3 Hours of light	4 Hours of light	5 Hours of light

Fig. 4-15. *Sample chart for recording data for project* How Much Is Enough?

Going Further

1. Do the plants that receive less light have less algae growth in their solution? Does the algae in the solution grow with less effect on the plant as the quantity of light is decreased?

2. Set plants up for the same periods of time but with an increasing distance from the artificial light source thus reducing the quantity of light they receive due to distance.

3. Can plants be forced to grow faster and more abundantly with greater quantities of light? Is there an optimum quantity of light beyond which more light or closer light will not improve the growth of the plant?

PROJECT 4-9
Hang Ten

Overview

The purpose for roots is to supply nutrients and water through the root system to the plant. Another very important purpose is to supply support. Can we teach roots to hold on to artificial support, such as a wire mesh or some other anchoring system?

Materials

- several seedling hydroponically grown plants (bush bean, morning glory, or others)—plants should be equal in size, health, and age
- 5- or 6-inch square of chicken wire

Procedure

Place the hydroponic plants in sunlight. Fold a five- or six-inch square piece of chicken wire at least twice, so that you will have one quarter its size (see Fig. 4-16). Do not press it together firmly. Leave spaces between the wires for the roots to grasp. Place the chicken wire in the test plant's solution, somewhat below the root system so that as the roots get longer, they will encounter the wire.

Cover the outside of the containers to prevent light from hitting the nutrient solution. Be sure to maintain the plants other needs equally (temperature, water, light, shelter from the wind).

Set up a log to observe the plants. Observe whether or not the chicken wire aids in support of the plant. See if the roots have wound around the wire to hold on.

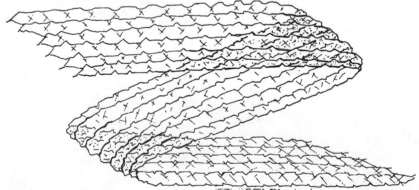

Fig. 4-16. *Fold a five- or six-inch square piece of chicken wire two or three folds to be used in training roots to anchor to an artificial support.*

Note: Hydroponic solutions can give plants everything they need and the plant might not develop large root systems. In order to make the root system grow more extensively, you might have to deprive the plant of some of its food. Thus, the roots will have to grow larger to enable them to get more food. To do this, all you have to do is use water rather than hydroponic solution every other time you feed your plants. It is important to change the solution at least every two weeks.

Your hypothesis as to whether or not the roots will cling to the wire in order to get greater support should have a time limit set, say about five weeks.

Going Further

1. Chemically evaluate the nutrient solution with the wire in it. See if you can determine chemically if the wire is causing a change in the solution.

2. Use a much smaller mesh wire where the openings are very small.

3. Using a wire with cheesecloth or burlap, attempt to anchor the plant through its root system without using a container. Only moisten the cheesecloth or burlap. Use a climbing plant such as a morning glory. String can be used for support.

PROJECT 4-10
Going Up? Going Down?
Adult Supervision Required

Overview

Radishes are a commonly eaten and easily grown garden salad vegetable. They have optimum pH soil requirements, as do all plants. Will they grow in a hydroponic soilless medium? What will be the best pH for them? How will "best" be determined? When dealing with a food plant, "best" should include taste and perhaps size and nutritional value too. In this experiment, we will grow radishes hydroponically using nutrient solutions with water of different pH values. Hypothesize that since plants generally grow best when the soil is slightly on the acidic side, a pH of around 6 will yield the best radish plant.

Materials

- 1 package of radish seeds
- 6 clear water glasses or jars
- 6 bottles to store nutrient solutions of different pH values in, such as plastic two-liter soda bottles
- pH indicator (either a pH meter, test kit, or litmus paper)
- pH increasing solution (either a commercially available pH Up solution or potash)
- pH decreasing solution (either a commercially available pH Down solution or sulfuric acid) WARNING: **Have an adult dilute sulfuric acid prior to using it—it can burn your skin. Wear safety goggles to protect eyes and protective gloves to protect hands.**
- distilled water
- dark construction paper
- vermiculite
- tape or rubber bands
- labels or masking tape
- marker

Procedure

Fill six bottles with distilled water. Distilled water has a pH of 7, which is neutral. Using either a pH up or pH down commercial solution or sulfuric acid and potash, make the six bottles contain different pH values, ranging from a pH of 4 to 9. The water in bottle #1 will have a pH of 4, #2 will have 5, #3 will have 6, #4 will have 7 (neutral), #5 will have 8, and #6 will have 9. To increase the pH of water (make it more alkaline), you can slowly add potash, mix, and measure the resulting pH. Similarly, adding sulfuric acid will decrease the pH (make it more acidic). Have an adult present when working with sulfuric acid. Also, have the adult dilute it prior to use. Always wear safety goggles and protective gloves. Label each bottle as to its pH value. Mix a hydroponic nutrient solution in each bottle. Use either a commercially available nutrient powder for general plant fertilizing or for special hydroponic applications. Each of the six bottles will be used to water and feed a corresponding radish.

Fill six glasses with vermiculite. Label each with a number from 4 to 9, representing the value of pH of the solution you intend to feed it.

You can germinate radish seeds directly in the vermiculite or on moist blotter paper first and then transplant the seedlings to the vermiculite containers when they get a week or two old (Fig. 4-17).

Pour a little of each pH-prepared solution into each corresponding glass. Pour enough to fill an inch of water in the bottom of the glass as shown in Fig. 4-18. The reason we are using glasses as growing containers is so that we can see how deep the water is in each glass.

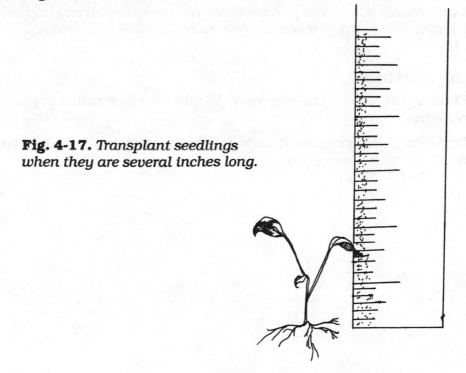

Fig. 4-17. *Transplant seedlings when they are several inches long.*

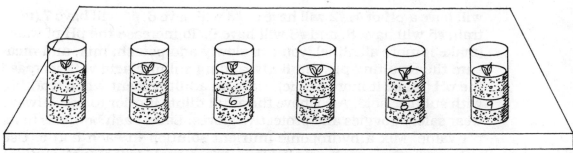

Fig. 4-18. *Determining the optimum pH for radishes.*

Using tape or rubber bands, wrap dark construction paper around each glass to keep light from reaching the roots. Place the glasses in a warm sunny area.

Every week, gently pour out whatever solution is left in each glass and replenish it with new solution from the appropriate solution bottle.

After several weeks of equal care, observe which radishes grew best. Because you can only fit one radish in a glass, you might want to have two or three radishes in separate glasses for each pH level. If you want two for each, then you would need 12 glasses. This would make a better experiment, because there is always the possibility that one radish might not germinate or not grow as well as another. The larger the sample test size, the more credible (believable) the results.

Going Further

1. Make a test of your backyard soil. Would it be well suited to grow radishes?

2. Perform this experiment using different vegetables, such as bush beans or house plants.

5

Stimulation

Many people complain that the high power lines that cross our country are problematic (see Fig. 5-1). Some people who live under them claim that they suffer from any number of ailments or that they have poor crop growth. It is true that a flow of electric current in a line radiates an electro-magnetic field. This causes an alignment of particles. Is there any truth to the tales that crop growth is affected by electric lines?

Plants respond to stimuli. Plants are mobile, but they move so slowly that we do not notice the motion of their leaves, stems, and roots. There are a few unusual plants that respond quickly to a stimulus, such as the mimosa tree whose leaves fold when the surface of the leaves is touched, and the Venus Flytrap whose jawlike leaf arrangement closes shut when a fly lands inside it.

Plant stimulation includes motion, electrical, radiation, sound, gravity, chemical, water, light, and touching. If a stimulus causes a response in a plant, it is called a tropism. This is a movement response, not a growth response. The behavior will either be a movement toward or away from the stimulus. If someone pokes your arm with a sharp pencil, you will probably move your arm away. Similarly, if you place a plant in sunlight, its stems will turn in the direction of the sun.

Fig. 5-1. *Some people who live under power lines claim to suffer from a number of ailments and have poor crop growth.*

Tropism name	Plant responds to stimulus
chemotropism	a response to chemicals
geotropism	a response to gravity
hydrotropism	a response to water
phototropism	a response to light
thermotropism	a response to heat
thigmotropism	a response to touch

Fig. 5-2. *The various tropisms.*

Tropisms are categorized by their stimulus types, as shown in Fig. 5-2. The categories are: geotropism, a response to gravity; phototropism, a response to light; chemotropism, a response to chemicals; thermotropism, a response to temperature; hydrotropism, a response to water, and thigmotropism, a response to touch. These factors occur naturally in nature.

PROJECT 5-1
Too Much Salt on the Salad

Overview

In order to remove ice and to reduce its slipperiness on roads, road crews use many different removal methods. Snow plows remove snow and ice while sand is put on roads to increase traction. Salt is also put down on ice to melt it. When salt dissolves, it creates a solution that requires a much lower temperature to freeze. Therefore, the process of salt on ice is really a melting process, changing the temperature at which water, which contains salt, freezes. Sometimes, road crews use too much salt and we find salt-damaged roadside vegetation. Salt can also run off into the storm sewers and create problems wherever it drains. Hypothesize that too much saltwater will adversely affect plant growth.

Materials

- 4 healthy house plants
- rock salt (Halelite)
- area where plants can grow indoors
- 4 gallon milk jugs or other containers
- measuring cup
- teaspoon

Procedure

Set several house plants in a window where the temperature will not be too high or too low and where they will receive ample sunlight. In three separate gallon milk jugs, mix different amounts of rock salt with water to create different strength solutions. For example, in one, pour and mix in three teaspoons of rock salt. That will be solution number one. In another gallon container, mix two teaspoons of salt. In the third, put one teaspoon of rock salt. Put the cap on the containers and shake well. A fourth solution will be simply water. Identify each of the different house plants as #1, #2, #3 and #4, with #4 being the control plant receiving only water (Fig. 5-3).

Water the plants using the appropriate solution for the plant. Stir the solutions before feeding them to the plants. Water normally and equally. Use a measuring cup. After two weeks, continue watering two more weeks using only water. Salt should still be in the soil and mixed with the plain water.

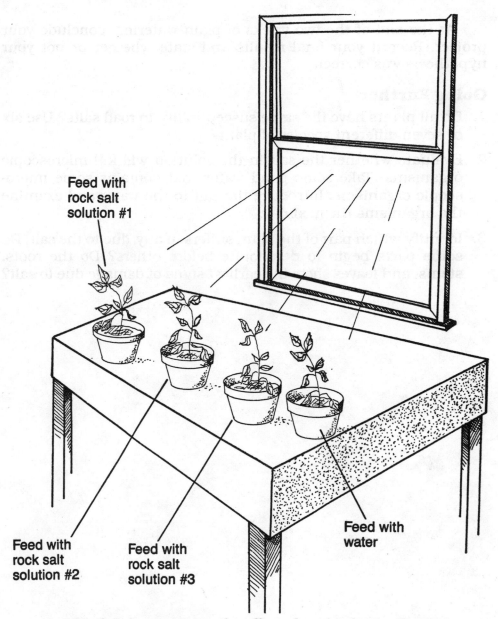

Feed with rock salt solution #1

Feed with rock salt solution #2

Feed with rock salt solution #3

Feed with water

Fig. 5-3. *Determining the effect of road salts on plants.*

Observe the plants each day. Record your data in a log. Hypothesize whether all of the plants receiving the salt solution will be damaged, or some of the plants be damaged, or will some do better than others.

At the end of the two weeks of plain watering, conclude your project. Record your final results and state whether or not your hypothesis was correct.

Going Further

1. Do all plants have the same susceptibility to road salts? Use six or seven different species of plants.

2. Evaluate whether the salt in the solution will kill microscopic organisms. Take some pond water that contains some microscopic organisms. Introduce the salt to the water and examine the organisms the next day.

3. Identify which part of the plant suffers, if any, due to the salt. Do some parts begin to deteriorate before others? Do the roots, stems, and leaves show the earliest signs of damage due to salt?

PROJECT 5-2
Hold Your Nose

Overview

We recognize odor through our noses through chemical analysis. Airborne particles of a particular substance reach our noses and create certain responses. Will plant root growth respond to chemicals that we detect as odors? Will the roots respond negatively, positively, or not at all (Fig. 5-4)? In this experiment, you will attempt to see whether odor produces a response in root growth.

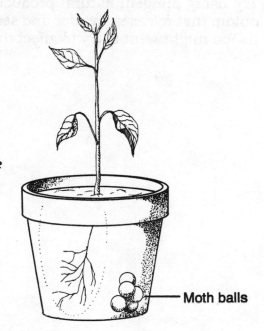

Fig. 5-7. *Mimosa leaves close when touched.*

Moth balls

Materials
- 4 healthy plants
- 3 ounces of mothballs or moth flakes
- some "cheap" perfume
- concentrated insecticide

Procedure

In three of the plants, place one of the three chemicals on one side. Use the plug system for replanting the root where a one-inch diameter column of soil is removed. The fourth plant will be the control plant. Set up a watering schedule. After several weeks, observe whether the root grew away or toward the mothballs, perfume, and the insecticide. Record your results then conclude how plants respond to odor.

Going Further

1. Are there other materials that you respond to because of your sense of smell that plants might respond to? Attempt to cause a response in a leaf or a flower using such chemicals. Soak a rag or paper towel with perfume and see if a nearby leaf or flower responds to the odor. Run the experiment for several weeks, soaking the rag every day.

2. Try using pungent natural products, such as ground radish or onion, that releases an odor and see if the plants are affected by it. You might want to try to affect the plant's root, leaf, or flower.

PROJECT 5-3
The Cube Root

Overview

Geotropism has a strong effect on plants. All plants detect gravity. How long does it take a plant to respond to gravity? Does the amount of light affect its ability to respond? Can plants be frustrated or confused? Form a hypothesis, then try this experiment.

Materials

- half gallon milk or juice container
- 2 pieces of 5″ × 10″ cheesecloth
- potting soil, enough to fill the carton cube
- 6 to 8 quickly germinating seeds, such as radish, lettuce, or green beans
- several rubber bands, staples, or thread
- masking tape
- string
- scissors

Procedure

Carefully cut the bottom section off of a half gallon milk jug or juice container creating a square cube (about three inches up from the bottom). Cut the bottom off too, so that you have a cube that has no top or bottom. Fold the cheesecloth in half and enclose the bottom with one piece, creating a doubled, five-inch square. Use a rubber band, staples, or a stitching method to secure the cloth to the carton.

Fill the cube half full with potting soil. Moisten the soil. Place the seeds in the surface of the soil. Then fill the rest of the cube with soil, covering them. Moisten the entire soil. Cover the top of the cube with another piece of cheesecloth in the same way as the first piece.

When you have completed this, tie string or tape around the entire cube from one open end to the other, leaving plenty of space for air to get in and for watering. Mark the four sides of the cube 1, 2, 3, 4, or A, B, C, D to identify them. The two open ends will not be considered sides.

Place the cube on one side (Fig. 5-5). Let it stay there for one day. The following day, rotate the cube to the next side. Each following day, rotate the cube to the next side. Rotate the cube one side

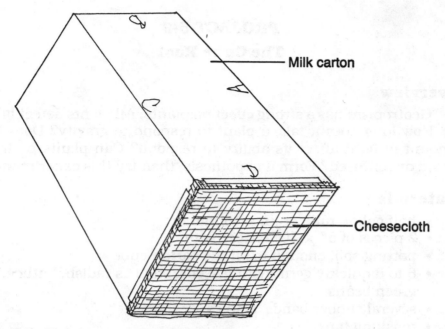

Fig. 5-5. *Construct a cube of soil with germinating seeds in the middle. Rotate it to a different side once a day.*

per day for 14 days. At the end of fourteen days, remove the cheesecloth cover and gently remove the soil until you get down to where the seeds have germinated. Identify the stem of the germinating seeds and the roots. Record your observations, then conclude whether or not your hypothesis was true.

Going Further

1. Use this same rotational technique using seedlings planted near the surface where the stems run through the cheesecloth. Rotate them each day.

2. Place the entire device on a rotating disk, such as one driven by a slow motor from an advertising display or a slow timing motor that moves with the speed of an hour hand, thus completing two revolutions per day. Observe and record data.

PROJECT 5-4
Just One More Drink

Overview

Plants need water to survive. They receive their nutrients in a water solution. They need to keep from drying out. Do roots grow toward water? Is growing toward water an important thing? The response of a plant to water is called hydrotropism. We might be able to detect the growth of a root in the direction of moisture in a small, planned indoor experiment. Will other factors come into play during this experiment? How can we control them?

Materials

- construct a growing trough or use a 12-inch long cake pan, 1 1/2 inches deep
- small wooden block, such as scrap wood or kindling
- several germinated seeds
- absorbent material, such as cheesecloth, sphagnum moss, or cotton
- small, 2″ × 2″ block of wood
- potting soil
- string
- vermiculite

Procedure

Fill the bottom of the trough or cake pan halfway with a 1/2 + 1/2 mixture of vermiculite and potting soil. Tie a piece of string all the way around the pan, from one side to the other. About four inches from the end of the pan (see Fig. 5-6) tie another piece of string all the way around from the other end of the pan. Underneath the string, place a half-inch layer of the absorbent material all the way across the pan. Fill the rest of the pan with potting soil. Place one end of the pan on the block so there is a slope to the pan. About one inch from the string up slope plant four or five seedlings across the width of the pan. Do this up slope with the lower string also, planting another four or five seedlings.

You are now ready to water your seedlings. The moisture retaining material will hold moisture longer than the regular potting soil. Place the pan where it can receive sunlight and allow the plants to grow. Sprinkle the surface of the pan evenly when watering. Water the pan the day after it appears dry. You will probably hypothesize

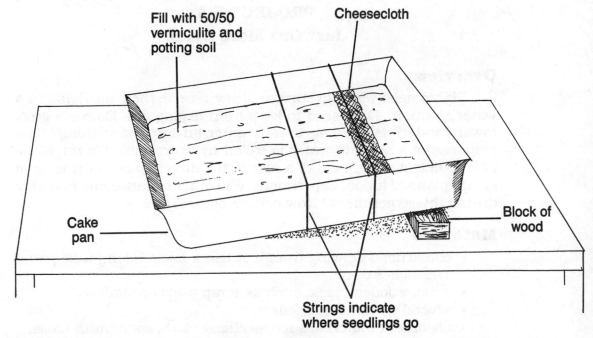

Fill with 50/50 vermiculite and potting soil

Cheesecloth

Cake pan

Block of wood

Strings indicate where seedlings go

Fig. 5-6. *This setup will determine whether roots grow toward a water source.*

that the water will run through the soil mixture and down to one end of the pan. The water going into the absorbent material will remain in the area longer, creating a well or reservoir for the plants. Will the root systems now grow toward the water or will they continue to grow in a widespread manner? At the end of three weeks, determine the direction the roots are growing by gently digging them up.

Going Further

1. Using a similar slope construction, use material (such as clay that does not allow water to pass) underneath the strings instead of using absorbent material. Create a reservoir of water that would be a larger water supply.

2. Use a wick system that runs down the length of the slope and determine whether the planted seeds that run perpendicular to the wick will grow towards the center where the wick material is and where the moisture is greater.

PROJECT 5-5
You're Tickling Me

Overview

Some plants or parts of plants respond to touch. Such a response to stimuli is called thigmotropism. Mimosa leaves close up when touched. How much pressure is required? Are some areas more responsive than others? Is the response greater or for a longer period of time if earlier in the day? Will it last longer or occur more quickly on a bright or warm day? Will light or time of day operate separately from each other?

Materials

- feather
- ruler
- pencil
- piece of very fine wire
- stopwatch or wristwatch with a second hand
- mimosa tree

Procedure

Establish a hypothesis, possibly one of the overview questions. Set up a data sheet to record your observations. Test the mimosa leaf (Fig. 5-7) with a pencil, a feather, and a very fine strand of wire.

Fig. 5-7. *Mimosa leaves close when touched.*

Establish a relative pressure by measuring the position displacement of the test leaf. Using a ruler, see how far the leaf moves away from its original position. Use the same distances for each of the testing substances; feather, pencil, and wire. The same area of the leaf must be touched for each test. Mark the time and observe the duration of closure if indeed the leaf closes. Record the results and conclude if your hypothesis were correct.

Going Further

1. Determine the leaf-triggering organism and their locations on a Venus flytrap. Will the Venus plant close if only one of the triggering hairs is touched?

2. Do natural organisms that come in contact with the leaf affect mimosa triggering, such as insects, birds, twigs?

3. Map out a leaf, expanding the size to three or four times its actual size. Use only the end of the wire or a sharp pencil to determine the points along the leaf on your map that cause the closing of the leaf. Hypothesize in advance whether these points will be close to the center line of the leaf or will they be far away? Will they be near the stem or more toward the outer edge?

PROJECT 5-6
Magnetic Personality

Overview

There is a magnetic field produced by the Earth, which can be measured. It has shifted and switched several times over thousands of years. There is something called nodes, places where the magnetic field is intense. Will this magnetic field or an artificially produced magnetic field affect the growth of a plant?

Materials

- 2 similar, healthy plants
- 2 powerful horseshoe magnets
- iron filings
- piece of paper

Procedure

Set up the separate healthy plants in a growing environment, such as a sunny window with little disturbance and proper temperatures. Check the horseshoe magnet for its magnetic field by placing a piece of paper over it and sprinkling iron filings on the paper. Establish and map out the pattern of magnetic field. Using the map, place the magnets around the stem at the base of one of the two plants where the magnets' intensity seems the greatest (Fig. 5-8).

Set up an observational chart. Observe and record daily. Maintain the plants with water and sunlight. To establish a more perfect control, you might want to place a piece of metal the size of a magnet, but which is not magnetic, at the base of the control plant. You could begin with four horseshoe magnets and demagnetize two. After several weeks, examine your results and conclude whether or not your hypothesis was correct.

Going Further

1. Set up a small electromagnet to create a field that surrounds the stem of one of the plants.

2. Set an electromagnet on a lawn in the presence of both grass and weeds. Determine whether the electromagnetic field has any effect on either of these species, and if so, does it have a greater effect on weeds?

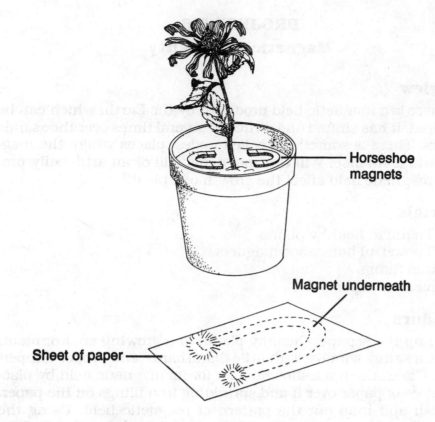

Horseshoe
magnets

Magnet underneath

Sheet of paper

Fig. 5-8. *Testing whether a magnetic field affects plant growth.*

PROJECT 5-7
Batteries Not Included

Overview

Electricity is a vital part of our lives. Our house is full of cables and wires, stereo and television cables, lamp and other appliance cords, and others strung all over the place. Do plants respond to electrical impulses? Will it cause them to grow more or to grow less? Some parts of plants might be better conductors of electrical impulses than others, probably relating to the water content in the xylem. This in itself would be an excellent area of investigation.

Materials

- 2 healthy house plants
- several pieces of wire, two feet long
- 2 batteries, preferably the large, square dry cell type (six volts)
- tape

Procedure

Set up the house plants in a good growing spot and throughout the experiment maintain them with proper sunlight and water. To the test plant, attach two wire leads, one to the base of the stem and one at the top of the stem. Be sure not to pull the plant over with the attachments. Tape the leads to the stem. Using two dry cells, wire them in parallel. Allow the current to flow for 20 minutes in the morning and again in the evening. Make your observations after two or three weeks. Reach a conclusion based on the results of your testing. Was your hypothesis correct?

Going Further

1. If the voltage used in Experiment 5-7 is too high, the plant might burn. Use a lower voltage and for a shorter length of time. At higher voltages, the plant would actually cook.

2. Using solid wire (24 gauge), insert the wire leads into the stem. Allow current to flow for 10 minutes in the morning and night. Use only one battery.

PROJECT 5-8
Picture a Fly

Overview

Some plants are in soils where nitrates are not as high as in other areas. Plants that adapt to low nitrate soils eat insects. They digest insects and utilize the nitrates in the insect to make up for the lack of it in the poor soil. Some *insectivorous* plants are the Venus flytrap, sundews, and the pitcher plant. This project will involve the digestion of an insect in the pitcher plant.

The pitcher plant holds a liquid in its inverted bell shaped flower, as shown in Fig. 5-9. The liquid is sweetly scented to attract insects. When the insects land in the liquid, they find they cannot escape. The solution then digests the insect. Does the insect, upon arrival to the solution, trigger the release of an enzyme in the pitcher plant or is it always present? Can we measure the solution in the plant to detect any chemical changes?

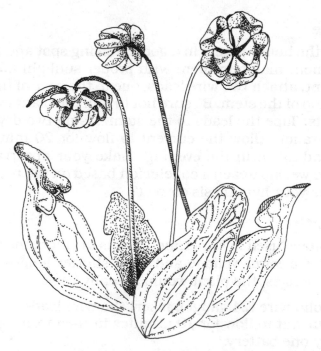

Fig. 5-9. *The pitcher plant eats flies and insects.*

Materials

- several pitcher plants
- live insects
- pH litmus paper
- nitrate testing kit
- cheesecloth

Procedure

Attempt to grow and maintain two or three pitcher plants. They require a lower pH than most plants and little direct sunlight. Observe whether or not the pitcher plant has insects in its solution. Using a piece of cheesecloth, cover the opening of the pitcher plant, allowing no more insects to enter. Maintain it in this covered state while you continue to grow it for three weeks.

This time period should allow the insects to be digested. Test the solution prior to the insects being introduced into the plant. Perform as many tests as you can obtain test kits for, such as pH, nitrates, and perhaps enzymes. After three weeks, perform the tests again on the solution. Record all of your observations and test results.

Place an insect in the solution of the first pitcher plant and record data on the condition of the solution for the next five days. Use the second plant and record data on its solution during the same time period. Was there a change in the pH, nitrate, or enzyme levels? Record all your data and conclude whether or not your hypothesis was correct.

Going Further

1. Feed your control pitcher plant a solution containing nitrate nutrients. Don't make too high a concentration or the plant might burn. However, attempt to supply its nitrate needs. Keep a cheesecloth cover over its opening to keep insects from going in. Run the project for four to five weeks.

PROJECT 5-9
Go with the Flow

Overview

There are plants that grow in streams. Does the rate of flow of water have an affect on the plant? Do plants grow more with increased water flow, or do they grow less?

Materials

- aquarium
- small electric water pump
- soil from the bottom of a stream bed
- 2 rooted plants from the bottom of a stream bed

Procedure

Fill the tank with the sediments from the bottom of a stream bed (Fig. 5-10). Transplant the plants from the bottom of the stream bed into the aquarium, each going at opposite ends of the tank. Put the hose from the water pump in such a position that it shoots water on the one plant but not directly on the other. A current flow is established by the water coming out of the hose, but it is not as strong on one plant as it is on the others.

Place the entire project in sunlight. Log observations over a two- or three-week period. Measuring the plants at the beginning of the project for length and total weight would help to quantify your results at the end of your experiment.

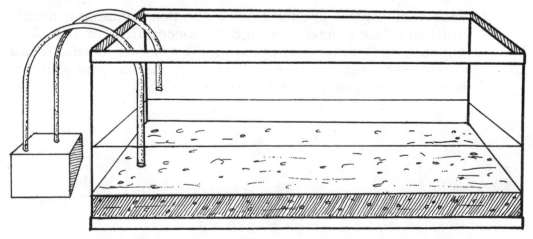

Fig. 5-10. *Testing the effect of moving water on a plant.*

Going Further

1. In a natural setting, quantify the length of plants on the turn of a stream, both at the inside of the turn and the outside of the turn. Establish some type of a flow metering device to determine differences in the flow rate on the inside and outside turns in the stream. Generally, the flow of a stream on a turn is greater on the outside of the turn than on the inside. Observe the plants for several weeks. You might want to tag plants with some marking device to be sure that you are observing the same plants each time.

PROJECT 5-10
The Hanging Garden

Overview

We have dealt with tropisms and other responses to stimuli. In many cases, though, we were unable to control other forces. In this project, we will attempt to determine which tropism has the greater effect, hydrotropism or geotropism.

In a water setting, all of the plants in or near water are affected by hydrotropism. Those same plants are also affected by gravity. What we will attempt to do is to build a project that will clearly indicate whether hydrotropism or geotropism has the greater influence on a plant.

Materials

- about four cubic inches of sphagnum moss
- 3 or 4 seeds
- piece of cheesecloth
- piece of string

Procedure

Make a ball of the sphagnum moss and wrap it in the cheesecloth. Soak it overnight in water. Implant seeds in the surface of the ball. Hang the ball in the air (Fig. 5-11). Be sure to keep it moist. A week later, evaluate which way the stems and roots are growing. Do the roots grow toward the center of the ball in response to water, or do they grow straight down in response to gravity? Record your data and conclude whether hydrotropism or geotropism causes the greater response.

Going Further

1. Will a hanging plant move toward a water source?

2. Will ground strawberries travel with their runners toward lower ground where there might be more moisture, or do they prefer to travel to higher ground? Observe a natural strawberry patch. Mark off its perimeter and observe the growth throughout the spring growing season.

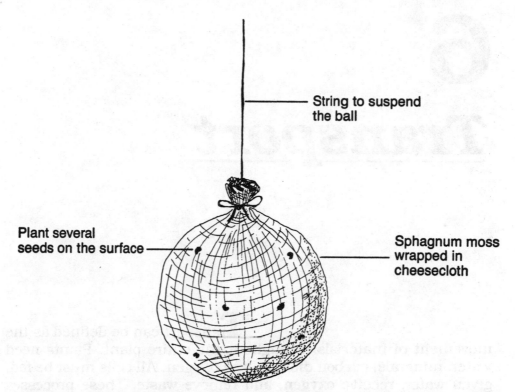

String to suspend
the ball

Plant several
seeds on the surface

Sphagnum moss
wrapped in
cheesecloth

Fig. 5-11. *Germinate seeds in a hanging ball of sphagnum moss to see which direction the roots will grow.*

6
Transport

Transport can be defined as the movement of materials throughout the entire plant. Plants need water, minerals, carbon dioxide, and oxygen. All cells must be fed, given water, receive oxygen, and remove waste. These processes must be continuous during any growth of the plant, flower, seeds, or fruit. Therefore, a system of transport must be available. In humans, the circulation system does the job by transporting blood.

Some plants are *vascular*, that is, they have vessels like miniature tubes or straws. These tubes transport (carry) large quantities of materials. If you live in a five-story apartment, you need stairs to get groceries and other items to the top floor and a way down to take the garbage out (an elevator would be nice!). Similarly, a plant must get water from the roots up to the leaves. Some types of plants, such as algae, mosses, and lichens have no tubes and materials must come in contact with the outer cells. These are called nonvascular. Experiments with these simple plants are covered in Chapter 7. Regardless of whether a plant is vascular or nonvascular, materials must be transported from cell to cell.

Movement of water in a plant is done through tubes called xylem. Projects dealing with the xylem involve transpiration (water leaving the plant) and respiration (water used by the plant). Food, in the form of sugars and starches, move through phloem tubes to be used by the plant cells or stored for future use. Movement of gases would involve leaf and root structures. Other movement would include chlorophyll in the leaves, pollen in flowers, movement from cell to cell by osmosis, and capillary action.

The quantity of material, distances transported, and seasonal differences will be investigated in this chapter. Effects of pressure, temperature, and sunlight on plant transport will be tested and experimented in the following projects.

PROJECT 6-1
Cover Up

Overview

If plants transpire at night, do they also accumulate the moisture for themselves, or does it merely evaporate into the air? The moisture that accumulates on the leaves must be taken up through the root system if it is to be reused by the plant.

We can measure one plant's use of moisture as opposed to another plant's use of moisture with evaporation taking place. Will a plant require less moisture if each night it is covered? This project might run for several weeks to determine whether or not the test plant requires less moisture than the control plant.

Materials

- 2 healthy plants
- marking tape or labels
- eye dropper
- 1 cover made out of plastic food wrap to be used to cover one of the two plants (completely enclosing and sealing it)
- tape to hold the cover together
- measuring cup

Procedure

Be sure all non-test aspects of the plants' growth will be controlled, light, temperature, and so on. At night, cover one of the two plants. Cover it completely with plastic food wrap and tape it in place. Leave one plant open. It will be hard to control the evaporation directly from the container unless you have a small opening container.

Each night, cover the same plant. In the morning, remove the cover. Shake whatever moisture is on the cover back into the container. Water the control plant every three days and water the experimental plant every six days. Use the same quantity of water for both plants, approximately 100 milliliters of water for a six-inch tall plant.

Construct a log to record your observation. After about 18 days, reach a conclusion based on your originally formed hypothesis.

Going Further

1. Will transpiration be affected by temperature? Will there be more transpiration or less transpiration in the evening and night hours, which are usually cooler?

2. Using an artificial light, maintain the experiment in artificial light. Provide a light at night. Will transpiration occur in the absence of night light? Note: Plants need a resting period and you might have to put the light out every other night.

PROJECT 6-2
Temperature Control Valve
Adult Supervision Required

Overview

Lowering the temperature of the petiole (the area between the leaf and the stem), reduces the rate at which food is moved through the petiole. If the petiole is restricted, will starch or sugar accumulate in the leaf?

Materials

- 2 leaves from the same plant
- Benedict's solution (can be purchased from a scientific supply house)
- iodine
- several ice cubes
- test tube
- test tube hand-holder or heat glove
- pot of boiling water
- measuring spoons

Procedure

While the plants are in sunlight, surround the petiole of one of the leaves with two ice cubes. Hold the ice cubes on the petiole for 20 minutes. After you have cooled the petiole, remove both leaves and perform both the test for starch and the test for sugar using similar parts in each leaf.

To test for sugar, put a half a teaspoon of granulated sugar in a test tube half filled with water. Using an eye dropper, put about 20 drops of Benedict's solution in the sugar water.

Fill a small cooking pot half full of water and, with an adults help, place it on a stove and bring it to a boil (Fig. 6-1). Shake the test tube and suspend it in the boiling water by using a test tube hand-holder, clothespin, ring stand setup, or heat glove. Be patient. When the solution heats up enough, you will observe a color change from the normal blue color of Benedict's solution. This color change determines whether sugar is in the leaf. The color change will be in increasing sugar:

green → yellow → orange

Test the second leaf in the same way.

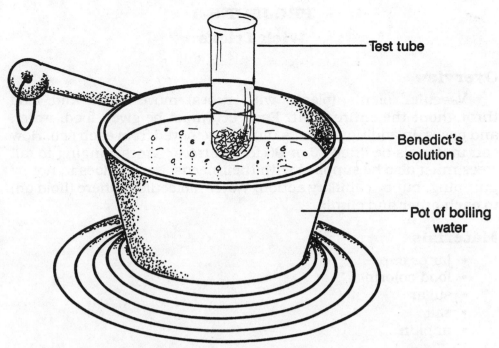

Fig. 6-1. *Alcohol is extremely flammable. Use this "double boiler" arrangement for added safety.*

To test for starch, put iodine on a broken leaf. A change in color to blue or black indicates the presence of starch.

Gather all of the data, then record and log your results. You might want to quantify your test results by the resulting changes in color.

Going Further

1. Can the rate at which food is stored in a root be changed by temperature?

PROJECT 6-3
Wick Tricks

Overview

Vascular plants (plants with tubes) move water and food throughout the entire plant. Each cell must be given food, water, and gases. In addition, wastes must be removed from each cell. How can materials be lifted 80 or 90 feet in trees? Vines clinging to tall trees must also be supplied with their needs. Nature does it, not by pumping, but by capillary action. Water molecules adhere (hold on) to each other and climb.

Materials

- jar or cup
- food coloring
- sugar
- salt
- napkin

Procedure

Wick systems can be demonstrated by filling a cup half full with water, draping a napkin into the water, and letting the napkin hang over the side of the cup (see Fig. 6-2). In order to come down the outside (gravity makes it come down), the liquid must first "climb" from the liquid to the edge of the cup. Will it carry sugar if sugar is mixed in the water to make a sugar solution? Will it carry salt, food coloring, or other substances? Use a clean wick and taste it to see if sugar and salt travel up the wick.

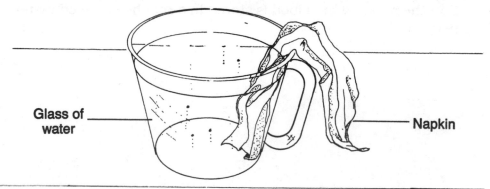

Glass of water _____   _____ Napkin

Fig. 6-2. *Capillary action in plants can be demonstrated by the wick action of a napkin and colored water.*

Going Further

1. Will increasing the temperature of the solution cause a greater flow or a greater volume?

2. Can the height be increased? Use taller containers.

3. Use different wick materials. Check for speed and total volume per given time period.

PROJECT 6-4
Root Pump
Adult Supervision Required

Overview

Water enters the plant through the root system. Osmosis (the transport of water through a membrane) occurs due to a difference in concentration of water. Outside the plant the concentration of water is greater than inside the plant. Therefore, water travels into the plant (across a membrane). This osmotic pressure is also called root pressure. Will root pressure lift water? If so, how high?

Materials

- 2 healthy tomato plants (can be growing outdoors in the ground or indoors in containers)
- piece of scrap wood or a book to support tubing
- sharp knife **(Be very careful with sharp objects.)**
- clear tubing, 2″ long, whose diameter matches the diameter of the tomato plant stem
- container
- candle or modeling clay

Procedure

Carefully cut off the top part of a tomato plant about four inches above the soil. Always point the edge of the knife away from the body when you cut—cut out. Attach the end of a clear piece of tubing and seal it with wax from a candle or with modeling clay. Do not use a candle without an adults help. Fill the tube with water and tap out the air bubbles. Position the tube to catch any water pushed out. Use tomato plant supports to hold the tube. Figure 6-3 shows an indoor setup. Measure the water gathered at various times of the day. Record your data.

Perform the same procedure on an equally healthy tomato plant. Do this second operation immediately following a rain shower. For indoor setups, change the watering quantity. Measure the water gathered at various times of day. Record your data and note any differences. Be sure not to let air into the tube.

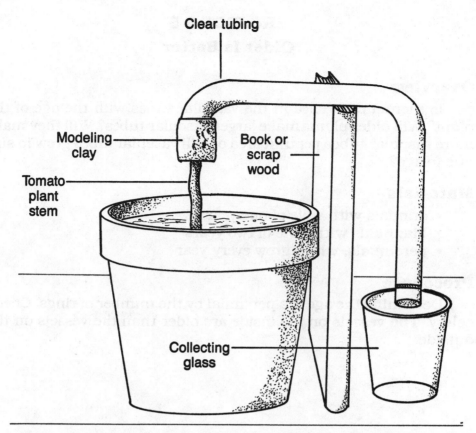

Fig. 6-3. *Root pressure can be determined by using a homemade manometer.*

Going Further

1. Try to inflate a small balloon using root pressure.

2. Use a naturally growing vine with two vines growing from one plant instead of a tomato plant.

3. Try to demonstrate root pressure using saplings. In the spring, food has to be going up the tree for bud formation.

4. Plants naturally use both root pressure and capillary action. At what point in the root or stem does root pressure cease and capillary action begin? Is it possible to find out?

PROJECT 6-5
Older Is Better

Overview

Is there a difference in the vascular tubes with the age of the plant? Will older plants make larger vascular tubes? Will they make more vascular tubes per unit area or will vascular tubes grow in size due to age?

Materials

- annuals with a life of one year
- biannuals with a life of two years
- perennials, which grow every year

Procedure

Determine the age of a perennial by the number of rings. Check celery. The vessels on the inside are older than the vessels on the outside.

PROJECT 6-6
Turn off the Water
Adult Supervision Required

Overview

If a plant does not receive water it will eventually die. If you break the flow of water in the system, that is, make a cut all the way around a tree, it will die. A cut all the way around a tree will not only break the water flow, but it will stop the flow of food. We have a tree limb over our house that annoyingly blows against the roof on windy days. If we cut half way around the tree on the side where the branch is growing, will food and water be prevented from transporting to that branch and cause the branch to die? (See Fig. 6-4.)

Adult supervision is required when using a sharp saw.

Materials

- tree (must have permission to cut it, perhaps an area near your home that needs to be clear cut or harvested)
- pruning saw

Procedure

With an adult's help, make a cut in the tree on a particular side. Be sure to cut in to reach the growth ring. In most oak trees, you would only have to go about a half-inch deep once your got past the bark. This is a long-term project, because it will take a few months to see if there is any affect. If you partially girdle a tree prior to the budding in spring, however, you might be able to make a quicker observation as to which parts of the tree are forming buds.

Be sure to record the time and date when you made the cut. Record the species of tree. Note that some trees do not grow in a straight line. Cedar grows in a spiral, so the semigirdling of a cedar might produce an affect on a portion of the tree that has not been tested.

Going Further

1. Can our offending branch be girdles, completely cutting it around the entire branch, to cause it to die?

2. Will damage in the root system on a particular side create a reduction in water and nutrient to that side of the tree.

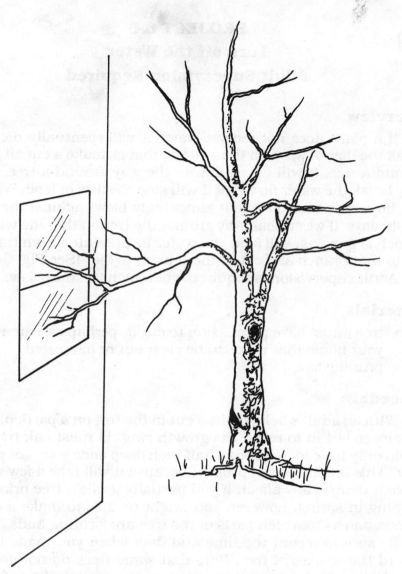

Fig. 6-4. *Testing whether girdling one side of a tree will cut off the flow of food to branches on that side?*

PROJECT 6-7
Bone Dry

Overview

Turgor, stiffness or strength, is caused by the amount of water in plant cells. Have you ever noticed that when celery is fresh and you break it, it snaps. When it is older, the cells have less water in them and the celery has less turgor, or firmness. Imbition, is the lack of water in a cell. Stems need to be rigid to support leaves, flowers, and fruit. Is there a way we can cause water to leave the plant instead of entering it?

Materials

- 3 indoor house plants
- area where weeds are growing
- 1 pound rock salt
- 3 jars or beakers
- masking tape or adhesive labels
- measuring cup (milliliters)

Procedure

Pour 400 milliliters of water into a container. Pour another 200 milliliters of water into another container. Add as much salt as can be dissolved. Pour 100 milliliters of this salt solution into a third container. Add 100 milliliters of water to the third container. Label it *50/50 Solution*. Label the first container *Water* and the second one *Saturated Salt Solution*.

Using three healthy plants, controlling all other factors (light, temperature), water each plant every three days using the three solutions you have prepared. One plant will receive all water, another plant the 50/50 mixture, and the last plant the saturated salt solution. Use 20 milliliters of water for each watering. Pour it near the stem.

Instead of using indoor plants, you could use three separate plots outside to water with the three solutions. You can also use cracks between concrete or driveways where undesirable weeds are growing. Select three areas of seemingly equal growth. Using the solutions, water them as you water the indoor plants.

Make observations and record your data. Your results might yield the conclusion that saltwater does indeed remove water from the plant, causing a turgor problem.

Going Further

1. Do some plants suffer more from salt than others? Will dandelions succumb before grass does?

2. Does salt contain any valuable minerals that plants might need?

7

Fungi and
Simple Plants

For our purposes, simple plants
are plants with very simple structures and functions. All but ferns
are nonvascular, that is, they have no vessels for transport of food or
water. Ferns are considered here because of their simplicity of form,
growth, and reproduction.

Nonvascular plants require water and food but have cells that
will transport materials through several layers. There are no tubes
(xylem or phloem). Therefore, they must be low to the ground and
in contact with moisture. They have no true stems, roots, or leaves.

Fungi are organisms that do not photosynthesize. They receive
nourishment from a host (living or dead material).

Lichens are combinations of fungi and algae. Each of these two
groups will be considered separately but also jointly in the case of
lichens.

Mosses comprise a large group responsible for ground cover.

Bacteria, viruses, and protozoans are not considered in this
book. They are best placed in the category of microbiology in science fairs.

PROJECT 7-1
Great on Pizza
Adult Supervision Required

Overview

Fungi are not truly plants. They do not use chlorophyll to make food. They must exist through the use or abuse of a host. Humans and animals eat fungi. We enjoy mushrooms in soups, salads, sauteed for steaks, and cut up on pizza pies (Fig. 7-1). Do mushrooms gather and store energy? The parts that we eat are the reproductive organs. Do mushrooms have a sugar or starch contained within them?

Do not eat wild mushrooms! Many are deadly. You can buy mushrooms in a store that are safe to eat and handle.

Fig. 7-1. *Mushrooms are fungi. They are not truly plants because they do not use chlorophyll to make food.*

Materials
- store-bought mushrooms
- iodine (use adult supervision)
- Benedict's solution (can be purchased from a scientific supply store)
- paring knife (use adult supervision)
- stove or hot plate (use adult supervision)
- cooking pot
- stove top

Procedure

Form a hypothesis about mushrooms, such as starch will be present but not sugar. First, test for the presence of starch using iodine. Carefully cut one mushroom lengthwise and place iodine along its interior length. Always cut away from your self with the sharp edge pointing out. Did the iodine turn a dark color indicating the presence of starch?

Next, mash up some mushroom caps and stems and mix with Benedict's solution in the cooking pot. Have an adult help you heat the mixture in a pot on the stove. A color change in the normally blue Benedict's solution indicates the presence of sugars. Record your results and conclude whether or not your hypothesis was correct.

Going Further

1. Mushrooms are not vascular. Research how they stand erect. Does it relate to rainfall? Find an area where mushrooms grow and count them. Count them in that area again after a rain storm. Be careful with wild mushrooms. Poisonous mushrooms contain microscopic spores that are hazardous. Do not pick them or kick them. Wash your hands after dealing with them in any way.

PROJECT 7-2
How High Is the Shelf

Overview

Bracket or shelf fungi grow on the sides of trees (see Fig. 7-2). The main part of the fungi (mycelium) is buried within the tree. It steals nutrients from the living host and is called a parasite. Each year it adds to its size. Some can be quite large having many layers. Are all species of bracket fungi found on the same types of trees? Are they species-specific? Is their place in the environment located at a particular height?

Fig. 7-2. *Bracket, or shelf fungi are parasites that grow on the sides of trees.*

Materials

- tree identification guide or book
- pad and pencil
- meter or yard stick
- crayon
- forest

Procedure

Form a hypothesis. Locate several bracket fungi in the woods and measure their height from the ground. Also measure the size of the fungi. Mark the base of the tree with a number. Log each number with height and tree species. After completing four or five logins, predict the next two or three. Photographs of the trees would enhance this project for presentation.

Going Further

1. Can you determine the age of the fungi?
2. Do they all grow in similar light conditions?
3. Have animals eaten any?
4. Do all bracket fungi occur on different trees?
5. Are sugar or starch present?

PROJECT 7-3
Better Than a Sponge

Overview

Mosses are small plants that have no tubes for moving food or water throughout the plant (nonvascular). They have no roots or stems and their leaflike structures have no veins. In some areas, mosses decay to form peat, which is used as a fuel. They also aid in reducing soil erosion by creating a ground cover to keep the wind and water from removing valuable topsoil. Mosses can hold water, helping other plants survive when rain is scarce. They grow throughout the world, from one pole to the other, from seashores to mountain tops, and in all soil types.

Sphagnums hold a lot of water. Just how much can sphagnum moss hold?

Materials

- 1 cup of sphagnum moss
- food scale
- water

Procedure

Measure the weight of the cup empty. Record the weight. Fill the cup with sphagnum moss and then with water. Let it stand in sunlight for about one hour. Turn it upside down to remove the excess water. Then measure the weight of the cup full of wet sphagnum. Record the data in a log such as the one shown in Fig. 7-3. To determine the weight of the moist moss, subtract the weight of the empty cup from the total weight.

Next, dry the moss in direct sunlight for several days (no moisture present). Then weigh the moss. If the cup is used, be sure to subtract its weight.

Compare the wet moss weight with the dry moss weight to determine how much water one cup of sphagnum moss held. Compare the weight of dry sphagnum to the weight of the water it held. What is the ratio?

Going Further

1. Determine which plants take advantage of sphagnum's water retention abilities.

Cup weight (moss + water) −	Cup weight (empty) =	Weight of (moss + water) −	Weight of (dry moss) =	Weight of water

Fig. 7-3. *Sample log to record and compute data for project* Better Than a Sponge.

PROJECT 7-4
Sie, Sie, Vitamin C
Adult Supervision Required

Overview

Many wild plants are edible. In order to eat wild foods, edible plants must be identified. Research will show which part of a plant is to be prepared and what to do to prepare it. All of the cultivated foods we eat grew wild at one time. Man has bred the plants to yield more or better food.

Ferns are edible. In early spring when they first "shoot" up, the curled-top leaf is called a fiddlehead. Fiddleheads can be stir fried or pan fried and are rich in vitamin C. Do some taste better than others?

Materials

- 2 or 3 dozen fiddleheads gathered in early spring (at least two different species)
- frying pan
- stove (adult supervision around hot stove and hot oil required)
- cooking oil
- fern identification book

Procedure

Gather fiddleheads from at least two different species of ferns. Make sure you know what they are before eating them. Have someone knowledgeable identify them, such as a science or botany teacher, park or forest ranger, or a park naturalist. Some plants are harmful to humans. Carefully cut about three inches above the surface of the ground. Always cut away from yourself. Wash thoroughly. With an adults help, fry one group of fiddleheads in a frying pan (around 350 degrees) until they are light brown. Next, fry the second group. When they are cool, do a taste test. Which do you prefer? Enjoy!

Going Further

1. Look for ferns with spores under the leaflets late in their season. Do the spores cover any stomata (leaf openings)? A low-power microscope is needed to see the spores and stomata. Do leaflets with spores have fewer stomata?

2. Check the stomata after long periods of rainless days. Use upland ferns. Compare to the stomata on leaflets just after a rain.

3. Test a fern leaf for Vitamin C content. This is done by mixing 1 gram of indophenol with 5 or 6 drops of ethyl alcohol. Dilute using 100 milliliters of distilled water. Use one-tenth of the solution in a test tube. Add fresh lemon juice, one drop at a time, until the solution turns from blue to colorless. Indophenol is available from biological supply firms.

4. Test for sugar and starch.

8
Plant Dispersal

Plants are found all over the face of the Earth. How can they be so widespread? They are transported from one place to another by various means.

The most basic dispersal is done by gravity. Many seeds are heavier than air, and therefore, fall to the ground, usually not far from the parent plant.

Lighter seeds are carried farther from the parent plant by winds. Wind velocity and duration become factors affecting the distance seeds travel. Pollen can become airborne and travel thousands of miles in the upper atmosphere. Pollen studies have been done with core borings in the arctic circle. Pollen has been identified from widely scattered parts of the earth. Prevailing winds and updraft regions will have a direct effect on plant dispersed by the wind.

The seeds of plants carried by water can be transported over great distances. Entire islands can be populated by mainland plants. The seeds must be strong and thick enough, however, to survive long periods in water. Floods carry topsoil containing seeds to new areas as does storm erosion and water runoffs. Water will carry anything along with it. Things that float will be carried much further. Different species can travel from one place to another by water currents, streams, ocean currents, and even in cities by storm drains.

Animals carry seeds inadvertently. Seeds become caught in their fur. They use seeds when building nests. Some animals bury seeds. Others eat fruit whose seeds are passed through the animal's digestive system intact and grow in an area far from the parent plant.

People carried seeds from Europe to the New World. There are strong laws today, however, about people bringing vegetation into the United States for the sake of the vegetation itself and concern over the insects and diseases it might carry. Topsoil trucking carries whole plants to new areas. Planters continue looking for new crops with which to make a profit. John Chapman (Johnny Appleseed) carried seeds into new territories.

Some plants shoot out their seeds. Other plants, such as strawberries, send out runners or underground rhizomes into ever-increasing areas.

Some plants reproduce by making bulbs. Where there was one plant having one bulb, the following season there will be two plants, side-by-side, each having a bulb.

In the tropics, orchids can produce as many as four million seeds per flower. However, each orchid flower does not produce four million new plants. The conditions where the new plant finds itself must be acceptable or the plant will not grow to maturity and reproduce. Oceans, snowcapped mountains, deserts, and other regions might have unsuitable environmental conditions for growth. Favorable conditions for orchids are very complex and limited. Therefore, of the four million seeds, only a few dozen might grow.

Finally, seeds can come to Earth from outer space! This is merely a topic for thought, but when moon rocks where brought back by astronauts, they were decontaminated to make sure that no organisms were arriving on Earth from outer space.

Some seeds are protected by fruits and by strong outer coverings. Some seeds are unprotected. An example of an unprotected seed would be a conifer.

Some plants live only one season. These are called annuals. They must grow and reproduce to prepare for the next generation before they die. Other plants grow during a two-year period, usually not reproducing until the second year. These are called biannuals. A third group of plants continue to grow from year to year. These are called perennials. A plant's environment will have a lot to do with how it produces seeds.

Can we measure the distances that seeds travel? In this chapter, we deal with the different mechanisms of plant dispersal, which allows continuation of a species. The seed is the new organism waiting to grow. Where it finds itself and how it gets there is the topic of this chapter.

PROJECT 8-1
One if by Air, Two if by Sea

Overview

The distance traveled from the parent plant will cause more rapid and widespread distribution of a species. Cones have seeds deeply inbedded in them. As the cone opens over time, animals can get into it to eat the seeds. They do not eat all of them. Some fall out to "fly" away. Will floating cones travel farther than "flying" seeds? Will a watery trip drown the seed? How far will the winged seed travel? There are several possible hypotheses. The largest project includes germinating the seeds of the cone.

Materials

- large bowl
- hair dryer
- stopwatch or wristwatch with sweep second hand
- 6 to 8 partially opened cones
- native soil and two containers
- water carrier
- tape measure, yard stick, or meter stick

Procedure

Open two cones and carefully remove three or four complete seeds. The seeds are small and lay up against the individual cone sections. Using a blow dryer, approximate the velocity it produces (Fig. 8-1) and make a note of the speed. Hold the dryer straight and parallel about three feet above the floor, then drop the seed into the air flow. **Never leave a dryer plugged in around water, such as a bathtub or sink. This is a dangerous electrical hazard.** Measure the distance from the drop point to the touch-down point on the floor. Use this distance and air or wind speed to determine distance from tree height to touch down.

Next, measure the speed of a local stream by floating an object from one point to another (a predetermined distance). Use a stopwatch or sweep second hand to find out how long it took. Record your data.

See how long and how well the pine seed floats. It must be washed up on a bank to germinate. If it sinks, it will die. Simulate the stream with a water container. Use a period of time based on

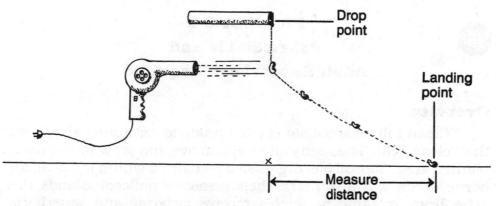

Fig. 8-1. *Use a hair dryer to simulate wind. Record the distances traveled by various types of seeds the same as they would be carried by the wind.*

stream flow to represent the distance from the parent, then place the seeds on top of soil and observe germination. Use several seeds in each group and water regularly.

Record all of your data on a chart. Conclude whether or not your hypothesis was correct.

Going Further

1. Will seeds germinate better if they are in water longer?

2. Is the soil near a stream more suitable for germinating seeds?

PROJECT 8-2
Baked Soil Island
Adult Supervision Required

STOP

Overview

"Clean Fill" wanted signs often produce vegetation along with the "clean" fill. The seeds and roots arrive and grow in the transplanted area. Topsoil has organisms contained within it. Local, airborne seeds will also make their presence noticed. Islands that arise from volcanic principles receive airborne and waterborne seeds. If soil is sterilized by baking it, will new vegetation begin to grow in it? If so, which species?

Materials

- roasting pan
- two 20-pound bags of potting soil
- flower pot
- slow running, shallow stream or creek
- kitchen oven (use adult supervision)
- 2 two-gallon buckets
- newspaper

Procedure

You can't fit 40 pounds of potting soil in the oven at the same time, so fill the roasting pan with soil. With an adults help, bake the potting soil in a preheated oven at 450 degrees Fahrenheit for 20 minutes. After 20 minutes, empty it on newspaper, refill it with more potting soil, and bake another batch. When all of the soil has been baked, let it cool and place it in the buckets. Fill a flower pot with baked soil and water the soil. Keep this flower pot indoors and water it regularly. This will be the control soil.

Carry the baked soil out to a shallow stream. Select a place on the inside of an easy turn (wide turn) where the water flows more slowly on the inside of a turn. Build the island about one foot from the shore in shallow water. Pile the soil up to create an island as shown in Fig. 8-2. Observe the island each day and record all of your observations. Also record any observations made on the indoor flower pot soil.

After several weeks, gather your data and conclude whether your hypothesis was correct or not.

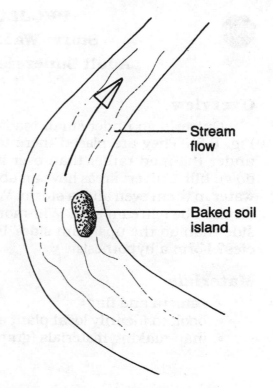

Fig. 8-2. *Put the sterile soil about a foot from the shore of a stream to collect seeds from water, air, and animal transport.*

Stream flow

Baked soil island

Going Further

1. Can you determine which species growing on the island were airborne and which were waterborne?

2. Did animals visit the island? Did they deposit waste (nutrient)? Did they bury any seeds or nuts? Did their body carry any hitchhiker seeds?

PROJECT 8-3
Storm Water Garden
Adult Supervision Required

STOP

Overview

Culverts go under small roads from one side to the other (see Fig. 8-3). They are placed there to allow water from storms to go under the road rather than over it. The direction of water flow is down hill. Culvert areas have an abundance of water and hold some water in them even after a storm. Waterborne seeds can accumulate on the downstream side. Will more growth be found on the down side than on the upstream side? Is there evidence of different species? Form a hypothesis.

Materials

- camera and film
- book to identify local plant and tree species
- map-making materials (graph paper, pens, ruler)

Fig. 8-3. *Culverts that go under roads can transport species of plants to the other side of a hill or embankment.*

Procedure

Identify two or three different culverts. Do not go near a road without adult supervision. Determine the direction the water is flowing. Make a small map (can be to scale if you desire) of each culvert area. On the map, indicate the plant species found and their location. Take pictures. In each culvert, were all species found on both sides? Using observations, and photographs, arrive at a conclusion. Was your hypothesis correct or incorrect?

Going Further

1. Can clippings or other parts of plants be carried by water to later take root in a new area?

2. Evaluate the soil. Does it contain more nutrient on the downstream side? Use soil test kits.

PROJECT 8-4
Thumb a Ride

Overview

Many plants produce seeds that cling to animals or clothes. They have hooks or barbs to grab and hang on. When they eventually fall off they might be miles away from the parent plant. Do all hitchhikers cling to or ride on all types of materials? How are hitchhiker species related, if at all? Form a hypothesis about hitchhikers and fur, cotton, and denim. Will each type of material gather the same type and quantity of hitchhikers?

Materials

- animal pelt/skin (such as a rabbit's fur)
- piece of cotton
- piece of denim
- local open field containing brush
- piece of rope
- small plastic bags (sandwich size)
- tape

Procedure

Tie the test materials to the rope, one behind the other. For example, tie cotton to the bottom, denim about 2 feet up, and an animal skin 2 feet above that. Drag the whole rope and materials through about 30 feet of open field. If you need permission to use the field, be sure to get approval first. Do not retrace your steps.

Collect and save the hitchhikers from your walk. Label plastic bags "1st Pass—Cotton—Bottom Position," "1st Pass—Denim—Middle Position," and the like. Be sure to remove all hitchhikers.

Remove the three materials and change their positions on the rope. For instance, put the animal skin on the bottom, the cotton in the middle, and the denim on top. Perform another pass through the field. Each pass should cover new territory, as shown in Fig. 8-4. Remove all hitchhikers. Count, bag, and label them. The last pass requires one more position change. Again, gather, identify, count, and label.

Gather all of your data and log your findings. Using the results, determine if your hypothesis was correct or incorrect.

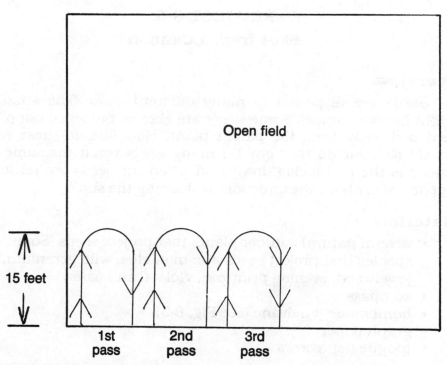

Fig. 8-4. *Make three passes through an open field, each time collecting hitchhiker seeds at different heights above the ground. Use different materials to see which materials best transport which seeds.*

Going Further

1. How long after the seed forms is it able to hitchhike and grow? The seed must form from a flower and be able to germinate on the surface of the ground when it drops. Can it wait a second season? Must they fall in an open field? Are they shade tolerant?

2. At what height are the hitchhikers on the parent plant? Will field mice, raccoons, deer, or all of these carry them? Do hitchhiker seeds fall when the plant is shaken? Allowing them to be transported by small, short animals?

PROJECT 8-5
Shot from a Cannon

Overview

Seeds are dispersed in many different ways. The strangest might be mechanical. Some seeds are shot or propelled out of the seed pod away from the parent plant. How fast do these seeds travel? How far do they go? Do many seeds reach the same distance? Is the pod facing downwind when the seeds are released? Hypothesize about the direction. Is it facing the sun?

Materials

- several natural outdoor plants that project seeds (Some species that project seeds are: mistletoe, wild geranium, jewelweed, evening primrose, violets, and pansy)
- compass
- homemade windvane (see Fig. 8-5)
- graph paper
- tongue depressors

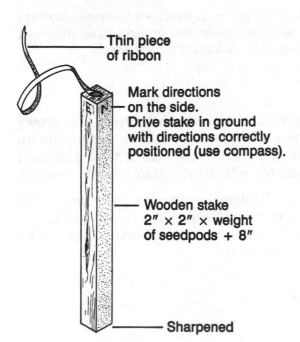

Thin piece of ribbon

Mark directions on the side. Drive stake in ground with directions correctly positioned (use compass).

Wooden stake 2″ × 2″ × weight of seedpods + 8″

Sharpened

Fig. 8-5. *To determine wind direction for the project* Shot from a Cannon, *build this simple wind vane.*

Procedure

Locate and identify a plant species that projects seeds. Find several and then study them. Gather information—when do the seed pods mature? Under what conditions are the seeds released? Does it occur at night? In bright sunlight? During a rain shower? Keep notes.

Set up a windvane at the height of the seed pods but not close enough to interfere with the dispersal. Using the compass, determine North and indicate this direction on graph paper. Mark a separate piece for each plant. Number them with a corresponding tongue depressor. Without disturbing the plant, place the tongue depressors to identify the plants. Clear areas around plants to enable seed detection. After pods have released their seeds, attempt to identify and quantify. Use the graph paper to record results. Be sure to match each graph to its particular plant.

Make a note of conditions, date, time, weather, and wind speed and direction for each plant's release. Compile all of the data on one graph and conclude whether your hypothesis was correct or not.

Going Further

1. Calculate the trajectory and velocity of an ejected seed. Use time, direction, and distance traveled.

2. Evaluate seed shape compared to other dispersal methods. Set up a display of "Seed Dispersal."

Sources

This resource list is compiled to give you a mail order source for seeds and other botany supplies. Each address has been checked for accuracy.

Seeds

Crosman Seed Corp.
P.O. Box 110
East Rochester, NY 14445
716-586-1928
    Vegetable and flower seeds.

Gleckler's Seedman
Metamora, OH 43540
    Large selection of standard and unusual vegetable seeds.

Landreth Seed Co.
P.O. Box 6426
180-188 W. Ostend Street
Baltimore, MD 21230
    Has been selling vegetable and flower seeds for 200 years. Big selection. Available by the packet, ounce, and quarter-pound.

Mellinger's Garden Catalog
2310 W. South Range Rd.
North Lima, OH 44452-9731

Sells mail order seeds, bulbs, plants, hydroponic plant food, and gardening supplies such as small netted peat pods for seed germination.

Stokes Seeds Inc.
Box 548
Buffalo, NY 14240-0548

Catalog of extensive vegetable and flower seeds.

Chemicals and Nutrient Solutions

Carolina Biological Supply Company
2700 York Road
Burlington, NC 27215
1-800-547-1733

Mail order firm selling complete line of laboratory supplies, hydroponic study kits and chemicals.

Peters Fertilizers
Grace Horticultural Products
62 Whittemore Avenue
Cambridge, MA 02140

Source for standard fertilizers, nutrient solutions, perlite, and vermiculite growing mediums.

Equipment

Edmund Scientific Company
101 E. Gloucester Pike
Barrington, NJ 08007
609-573-6250

Free catalog available. A good source for lab equipment such as test tubes, motors, and pumps.

Fisher Scientific
4901 W. LeMoyne St.
Chicago, IL 60651
1-800-621-4769

Laboratory apparatus, chemicals, water test kits, and hydroponic experiment kits.

Frey Scientific Company
905 Hickory Lane
Mansfield, OH 44905
1-800-225-FREY
Laboratory apparatus, chemicals, water test kits, and hydroponic experiment kits.

Hydro-Gardens, Inc.
P.O. Box 9707
Colorado Springs, CO 80932
303-495-2266
Equipment for those who are actively engaged in growing plants and/or produce for resale or research. Special low nutrient solutions for tomatoes, cucumbers, and lettuce which growers can add for desired nitrogen. Equipment such as bag culture growing systems, top spray automatic growing systems, and other commercial-scale watering systems available.

Science Kit & Boreal Laboratories
777 East Park Drive
Tonawanda, NY 14150-6782
1-800-828-7777
Laboratory supplies, terrariums, and hydroponic starter kits.

Sargent-Welch Scientific Company
7300 North Linder Ave.
P.O. Box 1026
Skokie, IL 60077
312-677-0600
Laboratory supplies and hydroponic starter kits.

Greenhouses

Texas Greenhouse Company
2701 St. Louis Avenue
Forth Worth, TX 76110
817-926-5447
Greenhouses for residential and commercial use.

Magazines, Newsletters, and Leaflets

Flower & Garden (The Home Gardening Magazine)
P.O. Box 5962
Kansas City, MO 64111-9983
Published bimonthly. Subscription $8 per year.

Horticulture Magazine
P.O. Box 51455
Boulder, CO 80321-1455

Hydroponic Society of America
P.O. Box 6067
Concord, CA 94524
Nonprofit organization that promotes and encourages national interest in scientific research in hydroponics by sponsoring meetings and disseminating knowledge through various types of publications. Bimonthly newsletter *The Hydroponic/Soil-less Grower*. Membership dues $25 per year.

Hydroponics as a Hobby
Leaflet number 423. Available from Rutgers University Extension Service, Dennisville Road, Cape May Court House, NJ 08210. An interesting and informative 16-page leaflet featuring an overview of hydroponics. Fee is $1.

Nutriculture Systems: Growing Plants Without Soil
Station bulletin number 44. Department of Horticulture, Agricultural Experiment Station at Purdue University, Media Distribution Center, 301 S. 2nd Street, Lafayette, IN 47905-1092.

Organic Gardening
Emmaus, PA 18099-0003
For the backyard gardener. Includes articles on gardening and health.

The Avant Gardener Newsletter
238 East 82nd St.
New York, NY 10028.

Eight-page monthly newsletter by Horticultural Data Processors. Subscription $15 per year. News and tips for gardening enthusiasts.

Additional and more detailed information can be found by checking with the following sources.

1. United States Department of Interior Office of Public Affairs, Room 7211, Washington, DC 20240
2. United States Department of Agriculture, Office of Public Affairs, Room 402-A, Washington, DC 20250
3. Smithsonian Institution, 1000 Jefferson Drive S.W., Washington, DC 20560
4. Botanical gardens (federal, state, county, local)
5. Parks (federal, state, county, local)
6. Reserves (federal, state, county, local)
7. Museums (federal, state, county, local)
8. Forest services (federal, state, county, local)
9. Special interest groups, such as garden clubs (national, state, local)
10. School clubs
11. Colleges and universities
12. Libraries: Use libraries to identify experts and their addresses. Also use the reference book *Reader's Guide to Periodical Publications.*

Glossary

algae—A simple plant containing no roots, stems, or leaves. It is the green material found in ponds or unchlorinated swimming pools.

asexual—Reproduction with only one parent. For example, growing an African violet plant from a leaf clipping.

Benedict's solution—A prepared solution used to determine the presence of sugar.

botany—The scientific study of the plant kingdom.

canopy layer—The leaf mass at the top of trees that create a layer of sun-absorbing material.

capillary action—Water molecules that adhere to each other. Capillary action in plants cause water and nutrients to travel up the tubes in a plant.

catalyst—A substance that assists a chemical reaction.

chlorophyll—A green substance that acts as a catalyst, in the production of food during photosynthesis in green plants.

control group—When doing experiments, a control group is the group that has all the variables maintained. For example, if you want to test the effects of carbon monoxide on plants, you must have two equally healthy plants. Both plants would receive exactly the same care and conditions (soil, sunlight, water). The experiment plant, would receive additional carbon monoxide. The other plant would be the control plant. The control plant receives maintained conditions while the experimental plant receives the variation.

corm—A thick rounded underground stem base and buds that act as reproductive structure, such as a crocus or gladioli.

cotyledon—The storage area in a seed for growth during germinates.

deciduous—A broad-leafed hardwood tree, such as an oak tree. Characterized by leaves that fall off at the end of a period of growth.

experiment—A planned way to test a hypothesis.

Fresnel lens—A lens that concentrates light.

fungus—A simple organism that does not produce its own food as plants do. Some scientists do not consider fungus to be in the plant kingdom.

geoponics—Plants grown in soil.

germinate—The period of time it takes for a seed to develop roots, stems, and leaves.

herbicide—A substance used to destroy unwanted plants.

hydroponics—A method in which plants are grown without soil. Plants are grown in a nutrient solution, sometimes with a soil-less medium to provide physical support such as sand, which provides no nutritional value to the plant.

hypothesis—A theory or educated guess. "I think when asked how much they would weigh on Mars, more boys will have accurate guesses than girls."

leech—To run water slowly through soil and dissolve out nutrients.

lichen—A symbiotic organism combining algae and fungi. The algae helps the fungi and the fungi helps the algae.

observation—Looking carefully.

parasites—Plants that receive nourishment from another plant but do not give any benefit to the host plant.

percolate—To drain liquid through a porous medium.

perlite—Porous pebbles, or rock. Because perlite has no nutritional value to plants, it is used in hydroponics as a growing medium.

petiole—The area between the leaf and the stem of a plant.

pH—Potential hydrogen. pH is measured on a scale of 1 to 14 which indicates the acidity (sources) or alkalinity (sweetness) of water or soil. A pH of 7 is neutral. Each number on the scale is a factor of 10 from the next value. Water with a pH of 5 is 10 times more acidic than water that has a pH of 6. Adding potash to water that is too acidic or adding sulfuric acid to water that is too alkaline, brings the pH closer to neutral.

phloem—Miniature tubes that transport food through a plant.

photosynthesis—The process green plants use to produce food by sunlight.

pollination—The movement of pollen grains from the stamen to the pistil of a flower. These organs can be on the same flower or on a different one. When a pollen grain unites with a seed located in the pistil, an embryo develops.

quantify—To measure.

rhizome—An underground stem like a root.

sample size—The number of items being tested. The larger the sample size, the more significant the results. Using only two plants to test a hypothesis that sugar added to water results in better growth would not yield a lot of confidence in the results. One plant might grow better simply because some plants just grow better than others.

saprophytes—Plants that receive nourishment from dead or living organisms.

scientific method—A step-by-step logical process for investigation. A problem is stated, a hypothesis is formed, an experiment is set up, data is gathered, and a conclusion is reached about the hypothesis based on the data gathered.

symbiosis—A relationship between two organisms living together in harmony. Lichens, for example, are both fungi and algae. The fungi provides the moisture and the water that the algae need. The algae provides the food that the fungi needs.

species—A biological classification.

stomata—The opening in the bottom of a leaf where it takes in carbon dioxide.

terrestrial plants—Plants that are grown in the ground opposed to plants grown in water hydroponically, or that naturally grow in lakes and oceans.

transport—The movement of materials (water, waste, minerals, oxygen) throughout a plant.

tropisms—A plants responses to various stimulation. Chemotropism is the response to chemicals. Geotropism is the response to gravity. Hydrotropism is the response to water. Phototropism is the response to light. Thermotropism is the response to heat. Thigmotropism is the response to touch.

tuber—A stem that grows beneath the ground, such as a potato or fern.

turgor—The stiffness or firmness of a plant caused by water in plant cells.

understory—The plant growth, low bush shrubs, and other vegetation that grows above the ground but underneath tall trees whose high branches and leaves form a canopy layer. The three layers from top to bottom are canopy layer, understory, and ground cover.

vascular—Plants that have vessels like miniature tubes or straws which transport food and wastes.

vegetative propagation—Producing new plants from the parts (roots, stems, leaves) of an existing plant. A whole new African violet plant can be grown by cutting a leaf and putting it in water. Roots and other leaves will soon begin to grow. Vegetative propagation includes cutting, grafting, and budding.

vermiculite—A naturally occurring mineral that contains millions of tiny cells, trapping air and water. It has no nutritional value to plants and is often used in hydroponics as a growing medium for physical plant support.

xygote—The beginning of a new organism in seed reproduction.

xylem—Miniature tubes that transport wastes through a plant.

About the Authors

Robert Bonnet holds an MA degree in environmental education and has been teaching science at the junior high school level in Dennisville, New Jersey for more than 15 years. he is also a State Naturalist at Belleplain State Forest in New Jersey. During the last seven years he has organized and judged many science fair projects, at both the local and regional levels. Bonnet is currently the chairman of the Science Curriculum Committee for the Dennisville School system.

Daniel Keen holds an Associate in Science Degree, majoring in electronic technology. He is a computer consultant who has written many articles for computer magazines and trade journals since 1979. Keen is coauthor of two books published by TAB BOOKS., *Mastering the Tandy 2000* and *Assembly Language Programming For The TRS-80 Model 16*. In 1986 and 1987, he taught computer science at Stockton State College in New Jersey. His consulting work includes writing software for small businesses and teaching adult education classes on computers.

Together, Bonnet and Keen have published articles on a variety of science topics.

Index

U

understory, 139

V

vascular plants, 96, 102-103,
    139
  age vs. ability, 106
vegetative propagation, 8,
    20-22, 139
Venus Flytrap, 73
vermiculite, 47, 139

W

water, 12-13, 73-75, 96
  distilled, 56-57
  hydrotropism experiment,
    83-84
  pH levels for hydroponics,
    70-72
  rate of flow vs. plant growth,
    92-93
  seeds transported by, 62-63,
    120, 126-127
sphagnum moss absorption
    rate, 116-117

transpiration and
    evaporation, 98-99
wind dispersal, 120
wind vane, 130
winged seeds, 122-123

X

xylem, 96, 111, 139

Z

zygote, 8, 139